Ahmad Shamlou

Elegies of the Earth:
Selected Poems

edited and translated from Persian
by Niloufar Talebi

 WORLD POETRY

Elegies of the Earth: Selected Poems
English translation copyright © Niloufar Talebi, 2025
Introduction copyright © Niloufar Talebi, 2025
Commentaries copyright © Niloufar Talebi, 2025

Earlier versions of the translations in this book first appeared in the following journals: *Asymptote*, *Catamaran Literary Reader*, *Los Angeles Review of Books*, *Caesura Magazine*, *The Markaz Review*, *Parsagon*, and *Vox Populi*. A selection was included in the anthology *Essential Voices: Poetry of Iran and Its Diaspora* (Green Linden Press, 2021).

First Edition, First Printing, 2025
ISBN 978-1-954218-39-0

World Poetry Books
New York, NY
www.worldpoetrybooks.com

World Poetry titles are distributed by Asterism Books (US) and Turnaround Publisher Services (UK). Subscriptions and standing orders are available from the publisher.

Library of Congress Control Number: 2025943371

Cover design by Andrew Bourne
Typesetting by Don't Look Now
Printed in Lithuania by BALTO Print

World Poetry Books is a 501(c)(3) nonprofit and registered charity founded in 2017 in New York City and a member of the Community of Literary Magazines and Presses (CLMP).

World Poetry's publications and programs are made possible by grants from the Poetry Foundation, Hawthornden Foundation, and the New York State Council on the Arts with the support of the Office of the Governor and the New York State Legislature, and supported by an affiliation with the Humanities Institute and the Translation Program at the University of Connecticut (Storrs), as well as individual donors and our subscribers. To learn more about supporting World Poetry, please visit our website: worldpoetrybooks.com/support.

Table of Contents

Introduction   ix

Fresh Air

Being   23
Fog   25
From the Wound of Abaei's Heart   27
Nazli's Death   33
Nocturnal (Many a Night Burned to Dawn)   35
Common Love   39
Farewell   43
About Your Uncles   45

Garden of Mirrors

The Flame of a Silent Fort   51
Garden of Mirrors   53
The Gardener's Dream   57
Fish   59
Poverty   63
Epitaph   65

Instants and Eternity

Genesis   69
The Capital of Thirst   73
Between Staying and Going…   77
Epic!   79
The Mountains   81
Reasons for Silence   83
Unfinished Ghazal   85
Nocturnal (He Who Knew)   87
I…Death   89
Nocturnal (The Alleys are Tight)   93

Aida in the Mirror

The Beginning   99
Nocturnal (Among the Eternal Suns)   103
You and Me, the Rain and the Tree   107
You and I…   111
…Death   113

Song of Our Meeting   115
Song of Praise and Worship   117
Aida in the Mirror   119
Tryst   125

Aida: Tree and Dagger and Memory!

Nocturnal (We Were Patient)   129
Nocturnal (A Bit of Evil in Your Soul)   131
...And So Began the Ruin   133
If Only   135

Phoenix in the Rain

River   139

Elegies of the Earth

Elegy   143
Hamlet   147

Blossoming in the Mist

Letter   155
The Price   161

Abraham in Flames

Nocturnal (There's No Door)   169
Nocturnal (If Night is Beautiful in Vain)   171
Nocturnal (You Didn't Just Happen to Me)   173
The Anthem of Abraham in Flames   177
Dark Song   183
On the Winter Within   185
To Die This Way...   187
Edict   189

Dagger in the Tray

Still I Think of That Raven...   195
Funeral Address   197
The Chasm   201
Song of the Greatest Wish   203

Little Songs of Exile

Children of the Depths   207
Little Song   209
Distance (The Seventh "S")   211

In This Dead-End Street   213
Tenderly (The One Who Says I Love You)   217
Nocturnal (No, I Haven't Carved You)   219
In the Moment   221
Tenderly (The World is an All-too-brief Way Station)   223

Unrewarded Eulogies

I Can't Help But Be Beautiful   229
I Didn't Want To   231
Grappling with Silence   233
I Wasn't Born Yesterday   243
And Then the Earth...   247
I Love You Without...   253
Nelson Mandela   255
I Wish I Were Water...   257

At the Threshold

At the Threshold   263
Still Life   271
Birth   273

The Tale of Mahan's Restlessness

Reconciliation   277
The Day After   281
The Sixth Song   283
Those Who Stand Vigil in the Night   287
Written in Dawn's Blood   291
When I First Saw the World...   295
Jagged and Endless...   297

Notes to the Poems   301

Sources Consulted and Further Reading   309

Acknowledgments   311

Introduction

I've thrown books at the wall for their authors' worship of Ahmad Shamlou. What sycophants, I thought, to so discredit themselves. But it's often exalt or erase in Iran—no in-between. Generations have been caught in Shamlou's gravitational pull. I, too, have been orbiting him for years. He's a Hercules of sorts. Half-man, half-god. His wife calls him her mythical man. The man created myths—of others and of himself.

It's possible to do an internet search and get the facts: Born in Tehran, Iran, on December 12, 1925, and died in Karaj, Iran, on July 23, 2000. Went by the pen name A. Bamdad, or Alef Bamdad, or just Bamdad, meaning Dawn or Daybreak. Stood blindfolded beside his father before a firing squad for two hours. It was World War II, the Russians had barged into neutral Iran, and teenage Shamlou had been caught in the tide of rapidly shifting political maneuvers.

This most erudite of cultural giants never earned a high school diploma. His father's military career dragged the young Shamlou to every corner of Iran—to all its peoples, languages, and customs—while exposing him to the harsh realities of a nation caught between modernity and feudal class struggles. Years later, he would channel the Babel he'd traversed into *The Book of the Alley* (*Ketab-e Koucheh*), an ongoing encyclopedia of Iranian folklore and the people's lexicon.

In the decades before I met him in 1980, Shamlou was imprisoned a few times, had manuscripts burned by the Shah of Iran's men, briefly toyed with and left behind the Tudeh (Communist) Party of Iran, and witnessed the CIA- and MI6-backed 1953 coup. Through the failed promises of the Shah's White Revolution of the 1960s and the upheavals leading to the 1979 Iranian Revolution, he steadily emerged as one of Iran's greatest poets.

Even amidst the uncertainties following the revolution and the rise of the Islamic Republic, Shamlou continued to create prolifically, ultimately authoring over seventy books, including eighteen poetry collections. He translated dozens of works; wrote essays, articles, and screenplays; recorded his poems in his deep voice; and lectured internationally. His writings appeared in numerous translations including French, German, Spanish, Swedish, Japanese, and Armenian, and in 1983, he was nominated for the Nobel Prize in Literature.

I was a teenager then, and he was the sun around which everyone at my parents' secret literary salons in Tehran gathered. I recall him abruptly retreating from our bustling living room, where he was holding court, into a bedroom because a poem had seized him, demanding immediate transcription. He brought not just classical music into our home, but also the arts of many cultures—from Greek to Chilean to Czech. Around that time, he had translated Saint Exupéry's *The Little Prince,* and was searching for the perfect child's voice to record an audio version. My little brother was briefly a contender. It was he who told me to read *One Hundred Years of Solitude.*

Shamlou had been unruly, a rebel. He staged a literary coup of his own, surpassing his poet-predecessor Nima Yushij (1895–1960), who had begun dismantling traditional forms. Pushing further, Shamlou helped drive Persian poetry into a new era, fusing humanistic ideals and radical literary innovations. A defining force in *She'r-e No* (New Poetry)—the modernist shift that revolutionized Persian poetry—he expanded its scope, forging a socially engaged literary voice that redefined poetic expression in Iran and helped push the movement toward full-fledged free verse. His epiphany came in 1949 when, after promoting Nima's much-anticipated new poem in his literary journal, he found the draft lacking in the innovation it promised. He let the publication fold, whether by circumstance or design, to avoid having to print it—a moment he called his rebirth.*

Translation was Shamlou's passport to innovations in world literature, which he imported and grafted onto Iranian poetry to fuel his literary revolution. He translated from many languages, often working

---

* Akraei, Behrouzh, and Ahmad Shamlou. "With the Bloody Pen Name of Dawn." Interview. August 11, 1992. http://shamlou.org/?p=2247.

with intermediaries or via a third language. Translation was more than just edification and pleasure—it was his laboratory for linguistic experimentation, which he harnessed in his own work. Inspired by Jean-Paul Sartre's *littérature engagée*, which positioned writing as an instrument of liberation, Shamlou embraced *ta'ahhod*, his vision of the writer's responsibility to language and society. Paul Éluard's poem "Air Vif," which he translated as "Fresh Air," clearly influenced not only the title but also the spirit of his first major collection, *Fresh Air*.

Shamlou's poetry was a clarion call for liberation: it framed poetry as a weapon of the masses and humanism as the bedrock of his vision, rooted in the belief that people had the power to shape their own destinies.*

A hallmark of Shamlou's genius was his vision to synthesize East and West, the classical with the contemporary, the high and low to invent language that propelled Persian poetry into the pulse of a rapidly evolving Iran. By updating poetry's subject matter, he transformed it into an urgent force that spoke to the struggles, hopes, and awakenings of a new century. Without sacrificing its depth, he democratized his literary mode, giving voice to the "everyman" in a range of registers.

I had prepared a lengthy introduction filled with biography and analysis, drawn from my previous writings about Shamlou. But let's get straight to the poems. That was his priority, after all. The epigraph to Shamlou's *Collected Works* declares: "My work is my complete autobiography. Poetry isn't just an interpretation of life—it's life itself." It's fitting, then, that this collection is organized chronologically, like a lifespan.

"Death" haunts many of his poems—not out of morbidity, but as a reflection of martyrdom, which, in the context of social struggle and guerrilla warfare, became a badge of honor for a generation reckoning with its scars. As Iran's twentieth-century chronicler, Shamlou bore witness to these wounds.

---

* Samad Josef Alavi, *The Poetics of Commitment in Modern Persian: A Case of Three Revolutionary Poets in Iran*, PhD diss. (University of California, Berkeley, 2013).

"Love" rings even louder. His third and last wife, Aida (née Rita Athans Sarkisian), was the perfect muse-wife-assistant-steward. The Aida of Shamlou's poems is both an invention and the embodiment of an ideal. She is an homage to the woman who took it upon herself to enable his work, a vessel for his grandest visions of love and humanity. Aida was a gift of epic proportions. After they met in 1962, inspiration struck Shamlou in the middle of the night, and lacking paper, he penciled a love poem directly onto the white plaster of his bedroom wall. "Aida in the Mirror" was published without a single edit. Aida said that in their forty years together, her feet never touched the ground.* It brings to mind Chagall's paintings of lovers floating above the mundane.

Ever the alchemist of dualities, Shamlou left even the intelligentsia grappling with the contradictions he embodied. A people's poet devoted to the everyman, he nevertheless rejected chauvinistic nationalism and simplistic notions of cultural pride. He critiqued Iranian art music for being frozen in time—a museum of scales, preserved yet untouched by innovation. A socially conscious artist committed to humanity's liberation, he also pursued beauty for beauty's sake. While resisting Western othering of the East, he also asserted an individuality that defied categorization within his own cultural tradition. A true nonconformist, he relentlessly pursued freedom—both for himself and for others—breaking through every constraint.

I attended his April 1990 talk at UC Berkeley, "My Concerns" (originally "How Fragile the Truth Is"), where his critique of the tenth-century poet Ferdowsi and his *Shahnameh* (*The Book of Kings*)—revered as Iran's national epic—was distorted. While he challenged its use as a nationalist tool, his sharp tone was seized upon to portray his remarks as an outright attack on Iranian identity itself, fueling a lasting rift with many Iranians. The threats to stab him that followed—courtesy of the

---

* Bahram Khazaei, "The Untold Memories of Ahmad Shamlou from Aida's Perspective," *She'r-e No*, July 26, 2013. https://shereno.com/post-18943.html.

very "proud Persians" he'd called out—only compelled him to continue his lecture tour, with UCLA as his next stop.*

Some twenty years later, standing on that same UCLA stage to present my translations of his poems, I faced wagging fingers and near-spitting rage. I couldn't help but recall the moment, all those years earlier, when I had stood backstage at UCLA, watching as Shamlou took that very stage.

Shamlou's legacy remains threatening to the powers that be in Iran. His gravestone in Karaj, west of Tehran, is a plain gray slab that sits in an aisle of identical stones in a crowded cemetery. It bears only his name, pen name, and dates. Earlier versions were repeatedly shattered and replaced with unassuming markers. The authorities in Iran prohibited a grander site, and official gatherings at his grave are banned. The stark and unceremonious grave is unsettling, yet visitors still come to honor him. Perhaps this quiet humility suits the people's "master poet of liberty."†

Happy birthday, Ahmad Shamlou. صد سال به از این سال ها —— *a hundred years better than these*. Here's to your momentous day, and your revelation to the West from your own one hundred years of solitude here.

On the Translation:

Translation is 100 percent loss and 100 percent opportunity.

On December 12, 2012, twelve years after Shamlou's death and on what would have been his 87th birthday, I picked up the phone to call his widow, Aida Shamlou, in Iran with a bold proposal: to bring this rebellious voice to the West. To translate Shamlou is to confront his artistry head-on. His work is vast and visceral, iconoclastic, and

---

* *Ibid.*

† Moslem Mansouri, dir., *Ahmad Shamlou: Master Poet of Liberty* (1992; Chatsworth, CA: Image Entertainment, 2000), DVD.

deeply rooted in Iran's cultural and historical milieu while bursting with universal power.

What began as a daring proposal turned into a thirteen-year odyssey. Along the way, I published *Self-Portrait in Bloom,* a hybrid memoir that weaves his legacy with my own coming of age around him and beyond, featuring early translations of his poetry. I also created *Abraham in Flames* (with composer Aleksandra Vrebalov), an opera for girls' chorus inspired by his influence, and delivered a TEDx talk about these interdisciplinary projects. Now, in honor of his centennial, this collection stands as both a tribute and a rebellion—a testament to a trailblazer who refused to be silenced.

Translators balance the demands of both the source author and target readers, shaping their approach based on factors like the author's recognition, audience, and existing translations. A modern *Beowulf* translation like Maria Dahvana Headley's, which starts with "Bro!," reinvents a well-known text for a broad audience, while more obscure works may first be preserved for scholarly study. Every translation falls somewhere along this spectrum.

For Shamlou, I sought a language of irreverence, one that honored his defiance without merely reinforcing the weight of the male-dominated canon he operated within. I wanted the English to preserve his rebellion against power and conformity. At the same time, I wanted to create openness, including the possibility of a female reading in a new era.

This task was especially demanding. The ambiguity, abstraction, and culturally embedded references of Persian poetry can feel foreign to English-speaking readers, especially to those familiar only with classical poets like Rumi and Hafez. I was also acutely aware of the uneven dynamics in translating an innovator from a "peripheral" tradition into a "dominant" language, where lack of context and familiarity shaped both selection and framing.

My first step was to fully grasp the poems—their context, layers, and evolving interpretations—guided by patient mentors. The challenge was to render this formidable voice into a form that resonates with contemporary readers while preserving its cultural specificity. It meant reimagining the sociopolitical urgency of his era, when poetry was central to public life, for a world where it has been pushed to the margins. The rise of anti-intellectualism, extreme individualism, and distraction-driven media keep us distanced from poetry's power to incite change and collective catharsis. Yet, we all hunger for it. In other words, the task was to offer Shamlou to the age of hyper-speed content without stripping his gravitas.

Months before submitting the manuscript, my translations still carried a distinctly mid-twentieth-century English tone. At this pivotal moment, I—the bilingual, bicultural mediator—had to relinquish how I "heard" Shamlou in English, still suspended between two languages. The poems had to move beyond me and stand on their own. Contemporizing them was emotionally grueling, like losing something while grasping for what remained just out of reach.

Inspired by Shamlou's adaptive approach, I prioritized flow and musicality, adjusting literal or chronological renderings that disrupted the rhythm and sonic pleasure of English. Persian punctuation is less standardized than English, allowing for more flexible and varied use. In translation, I streamlined punctuation to enhance clarity and align with English conventions and the intentions of the text. In transliteration, I omitted diacritics that distinguish between short and long vowels for readability and accessibility. When words or idioms carried cultural, philosophical, or religious significance that defied direct translation, I either kept them with explanatory notes or used the closest English equivalents.

Translating the poems guided by these priorities meant dismantling and rebuilding them. I lifted layers until the subversive energy of his poems spoke in a modern register. As the translations found their own voice in English, they began to feel familiar and alive. Like they were finally—after a lengthy, messy, and doubt-ridden process—reborn.

On the Sources and Selections:

For this selection, I consulted multiple editions of *The Collected Works of Ahmad Shamlou*,* analyzing discrepancies, accounting for potential proofreading errors, and cross-referencing them with Shamlou's audio recordings and an official timeline prepared by Aida Shamlou. The Persian text maintains Shamlou's unique orthography. I curated selections from across his oeuvre, excluding the first four of his eighteen collections, which he didn't consider part of his mature body of work.

To capture the breadth of his stylistic transformations, I selected poems that showcase his major forms—love poems, scriptural reimaginings, politically charged works, intimate first-person reflections, and experiments with both high and low registers—spanning his four creative eras:

1. The Transitional Period (late 1940s–early 1950s): Influenced by *She'r-e Nimaa'i* (Nimaic Poetry, named after Nima Yushij, which retained some classical elements, such as meter, but allowed for flexibility in line length and rhyme schemes), Shamlou began breaking traditional forms in *Forgotten Songs* (published posthumously), *23*, *Manifesto*, and *Irons and Feelings*.
2. The Experimental Period (mid-1950s–mid-1960s): Shamlou broke linguistic conventions yet maintained musicality, pioneered *She'r-e Sepid* ("White Poetry," or free verse) and forged his distinctive voice in *Fresh Air*, *Garden of Mirrors*, *Instants and Eternity*, *Aida in the Mirror*, and *Aida: Tree, Dagger, and Memory!*, blending in colloquial registers and honing themes of universal love.
3. The Transformed Period (mid-1960s–early 1980s): Leading up to the 1979 revolution, Shamlou became an outward-facing poet with socially resonant works such as *Phoenix in the Rain*, *Elegies of the Earth*, *Blossoming in the Mist*, *Abraham in Flames*, *Dagger in the Tray*, and *Little Songs of Exile*.

---

* Ahmad Shamlou, *Majmou'e-ye Asar-e Ahmad Shamlou* [The Collected Works of Ahmad Shamlou]. Vol. 1. Tehran: Negah Publishing, 2004 [5th ed.]; 2010 [9th ed.].

4. The Reflective Period (post-1979–2000): Shamlou's poetry became more existential, as seen in *Unrewarded Eulogies*, *At the Threshold*, and *The Tale of Mahan's Restlessness*.

Structurally, this collection follows his publication chronology, though a few poems deviate from their original sequence to help readers engage with the progression of themes and styles.

At the end of this long labor, I emerge transformed by a lifelong entanglement that reshaped how I think, create, and exist in the world. Despite Shamlou's extraordinary achievements, he remains far less known internationally than poets like Neruda, for example. My hope is that one day his work will be widely translated, allowing for rich comparative studies and critical editions in English. May this volume move Shamlou's new readers as he did me.

Niloufar Talebi
March 2025, San Francisco

Elegies of the Earth

Selected Poems

هوایِ تازه
۱۳۳۶

Fresh Air

1957

بودن

گر بدین‌سان زیست باید پَست
من چه بی شرمام اگر فانوسِ عمرم را به رسوائی نیاویزم
بر بلندِ کاجِ خشکِ کوچه‌یِ بن‌بست.

گر بدین‌سان زیست باید پاک
من چه ناپاک‌ام اگر نَنْشانم از ایمانِ خود، چون کوه
یادگاریْ جاودانه، بر ترازِ بی‌بقایِ خاک.

۱۳۳۲

Being

If life must be lived this lowly
how shameful of me not to hang the lamp of my life
high on the dry pine of a dead-end road.

If life must be lived this purely
how impure of me not to leave an eternal mark of my faith,
like a mountain,
on the fleeting face of the earth.

   1953

مِه

بیابان را، سراسر، مه گرفته‌ست.
چراغ قریه پنهان است
موجی گرم در خونِ بیابان است
بیابان، خسته
لب بسته
نفس بشکسته
در هذیانِ گرم مه، عرق می‌ریزدش آهسته از هر بند.

«‌– بیابان را سراسر مه گرفته‌ست. [می‌گوید به خود، عابر]
سگانِ قریه خاموش‌اند.
در شولای مه پنهان، به خانه می‌رسم. **گل‌کو** نمی‌داند. مرا ناگاه در درگاه می‌بیند، به چشم‌اش قطره اشکی بر لب‌اش لب‌خند، خواهد گفت:
«‌– بیابان را سراسر مه گرفته‌ست... با خود فکر می‌کردم که مه گر هم‌چنان تا صبح می‌پائید مردانِ جسور از خفیه‌گاهِ خود به دیدارِ عزیزان بازمی‌گشتند.»

□

بیابان را
سراسر
مه گرفته‌ست.
چراغ قریه پنهان است، موجی گرم در خونِ بیابان است.
بیابانَ – خسته لب بسته نفس بشکسته در هذیانِ گرم مه عرق می‌ریزدش آهسته از هر بند...

۱۳۳۲

Fog

The desert is all in a fog
The village light is hidden
A warm ripple runs in the desert's blood
The desert, worn out,
    silent-lipped
        and breathless
            slowly sweats from every seam in a feverish haze of fog.

The passerby thinks: "The desert is all in a fog. The village dogs are quiet. Wrapped in a thick shroud of fog, I reach home. Golku doesn't know. She'll spot me in the doorway, a tear in her eye, a smile on her lips, and she'll say:
The desert is all in a fog…I was just thinking, if it holds until dawn, the brave will come out of hiding to see their loved ones."

    ☐

The desert
    is all
        in a fog
The village light is hidden. A warm ripple runs in the desert's blood.
The desert, worn out, silent-lipped and breathless, slowly sweats from
  every seam
        in a feverish haze of fog…

1953

از زخمِ قلبِ «آبائی»

دخترانِ دشت!
دخترانِ انتظار!
دخترانِ امیدِ تنگ
    در دشتِ بی‌کران،
    و آرزوهایِ بی‌کران
    در خُلق‌هایِ تنگ!
دخترانِ خیالِ آلاچیقِ نو
در آلاچیق‌هایی که صد سال! –

از زرهِ جامه‌تان اگر بشکوفید
    بادِ دیوانه
یالِ بلندِ اسبِ تمنا را
آشفته کرد خواهد...

☐

دخترانِ رودِ گِل‌آلود!
دخترانِ هزار ستونِ شعله به تاقِ بلندِ دود!
دخترانِ عشق‌هایِ دور
    روزِ سکوت و کار
    شب‌هایِ خسته‌گی!

دخترانِ روز
    بی‌خسته‌گی دویدن،
شب
    سرشکسته‌گی! –

در باغِ راز و خلوتِ مردِ کدام عشق –
در رقصِ راهبانه‌یِ شکرانه‌یِ کدام
    آتش‌زدایِ کام
بازوانِ فواره‌یی‌تان را
    خواهید برفراشت؟

☐

From the Wound of Abaei's Heart

Daughters of the plain!
Daughters of longing!
Daughters of narrow hope
                        in boundless plains
and boundless dreams
                        in narrow spirits!
Daughters dreaming of a new arbor
                        in arbors a hundred years old!—

If you blossom out of the armor of your dress
the mad wind
will tousle the long mane
of the horse of desire...

☐

Daughters of the muddy river!
Daughters of a thousand pillars of fire up to the dome of smoke!
Daughters of distant loves,
                  of days of silence and slog,
                                of nights of exhaustion!
Daughters of running tirelessly
                  by day
                        and of broken spirits
                                    at night!—

In whose secret garden, in the intimacy of which lover,
                                for which blissful release
in a devout dance of gratitude
                      will you raise your fountain arms?

☐

افسوس!
موها، نگاه‌ها
بهعبث
عطرِ لغاتِ شاعر را تاریک می‌کنند.

دخترانِ رفت‌وآمد
در دشتِ مه‌زده!
دخترانِ شرم
شبنم
افتادگی
– رمه! –

از زخمِ قلبِ **آبائی**
در سینه‌ی کدامِ شما خون چکیده است؟
پستان‌تان، کدامِ شما
گُل داده در بهارِ بلوغ‌اش؟
لب‌هایِ‌تان کدامِ شما
لب‌هایِ‌تان کدام
– بگوئید! –
در کامِ او شکفته، نهان، عطرِ بوسه‌ئی؟

شب‌هایِ تارِ نم‌نمِ باران – که نیست کار –
اکنون کدام یک زِ شما
بیدار می‌مانید
در بسترِ خشونتِ نومیدی
در بسترِ فشرده‌ی دل‌تنگی
در بسترِ تفکرِ پُردردِ رازِتان
تا یادِ آن – که خشم و جسارت بود –
بدرخشاند
تا دیرگاه، شعله‌ی آتش را
در چشمِ بازِتان؟

□

بینِ شما کدام
– بگوئید! –

Alas!
Tousled hair and glances try
                in vain
to overshadow the poet's fragrant words.

Daughters of repeated rounds
                to and from the misty plain!
Daughters of modesty
        of dewdrops,
                of humility
                        and the herd!—
Whose chest among you has taken the blood that drips
from the wound of Abaei's heart?
Whose breast among you
has bloomed in the spring of his youth?
Whose lips among you,
whose lips—
        tell me!—
have secretly planted a fragrant kiss into his mouth?

On hazy, drizzling nights, when there is no work,
who among you lies awake
on a bed of cruel despair,
a bed of crushed desires,
of bitter brooding over your secret,
as the memory of him—who was all courage and rage
                        —sparks a flame
late into the night
in your open eyes?

    ☐

Who among you—
        tell me!—

بین شما کدام
صیَقل می‌دهید
سلاحِ آبائی را
براي
روزِ
انتقام؟

۱۳۳۰
ترکمن صحرا - اوبه‌يِ سُفلی

who among you

is polishing

Abaei's sword

      for the day

           of reckoning?

1951
Turkmen Sahra, Lower Owbeh

مرگِ «نازلی»

در خاموشیِ وارتان سالاخانیان

«- **نازلی**! بهار خنده زد و ارغوان شکفت،
در خانه، زیر پنجره گُل داد یاسِ پیر.
دست از گمان بدار!
با مرگِ نحس پنجه میفکن!
بودن به از نبود شدن، خاصه در بهار...»

نازلی سخن نگفت،
    سرافراز
دندانِ خشم بر جگرِ خسته بست و رفت...

◻

« - **نازلی**! سخن بگو!
مرغِ سکوت، جوجه‌یِ مرگی فجیع را
در آشیان به بیضه نشسته‌ست!»

نازلی سخن نگفت؛
    چو خورشید
از تیره‌گی برآمد و در خون نشست و رفت...

◻

نازلی سخن نگفت
نازلی ستاره بود
یک دَم درین ظلام درخشید و جَست و رفت...

نازلی سخن نگفت
نازلی بنفشه بود
گُل داد و
مژده داد: «زمستان شکسته‌ست!»
   و
    رفت...

۱۳۳۳
زندانِ قصر

Nazli's Death

On the silencing of Vartan Salakhanian

"Nazli! Springtime smiled, redbuds bloomed,
the old jasmine finally flowered underneath the windowsill.
Let go of your doubts!
Stop wrestling with ominous death!
It's better to be than to be undone—most of all in the spring..."

Nazli said nothing.
                Head held high,
he clenched his furious teeth into his wounded spleen and left...

   ☐

"Nazli! Say something!
The bird of silence has laid the egg
of a brutal death in its nest!"

Nazli said nothing.
                Like the sun,
he rose from darkness, sank into blood and left...

   ☐

Nazli said nothing
Nazli was a star:
for a moment, he flared in the darkness, leaped and left...

Nazli said nothing
Nazli was a violet:
he flowered
        and declared: *Winter has broken!*
                              and then,
                                          he was gone...

    1954
    Qasr prison

شبانه (وه! چه شب‌هایِ سحرسوخته)

وه! چه شب‌هایِ سحرسوخته
من
خسته
در بسترِ بی‌خوابیِ خویش
درِ بی‌پاسخ ویرانه‌یِ هر خاطره را کز تو در آن
یادگاری به نشان داشته‌ام کوفته‌ام.

کس نپرسید ز کوبنده ولیک
با صدایِ تو که می‌پیچد در خاطرِ من:
«ــ کیست کوبنده‌یِ در؟»

هیچ در باز نشد
تا خطوطِ گُم و رؤیائیِ رُخسارِ تو را
بازیابم من یک بارِ دگر...

آه! تنها همه جا، از تکِ تاریک، فراموشیِ کور
سویِ من داد آواز
پاسخی کوته و سرد:
«ــ مُرد دل‌بندِ تو، مَرد!»

◻︎

راست است این سخنان:
من چنان آینه‌وار
در نظرگاهِ تو اِستادم پاک،
که چو رفتی زِ برم
چیزی از ماحصلِ عشقِ تو بر جای نمانْد
در خیال و نظرم
غیرِ اندوهی در دل، غیرِ نامی به زبان،
جزِ خطوطِ گُم و ناپیدائی
در رسوبِ غمِ روزان و شبان...

◻︎

لیک ازین فاجعه‌یِ ناباور

Nocturnal (Many a Night Burned to Dawn)

Many a night burned to dawn
                      when,
tired in my sleepless bed,
I knocked on the desolate ruins of each memory
I'd marked with a keepsake from you.

No one asked who's knocking and yet,
your voice echoes in my mind—
Who's that knocking?

No door opened
to let me find once more
the lost, dreamlike lines of your face...

Only blind oblivion called out to me
from every dark abyss—
a cold, blunt reply:
Your beloved's gone, man.

    ☐

These words ring true:
Pure as a mirror, I stood before you
so that when you left my side
nothing remained in my mind's eye
of the fruits of your love,
but a heartache, a name on the tongue,
lost, invisible lines
in the silt of circadian sorrows...

    ☐

Yet, since this unthinkable tragedy—
with the cry that spilled at the untimely sight of you
flooding the stillness of my hallway of forgetfulness—

با غریوی که
ز دیدارِ به ناهنگام‌ات
ریخت در خلوت و خاموشی‌یِ دهلیزِ فراموشی‌یِ من،
در دلِ آینه
باز
سایه می‌گیرد رنگ
در اتاقِ تاریک
شبحی می‌کشد از پنجره سر،
در اجاقِ خاموش
شعله‌ئی می‌جهد از خاکستر.

□

من درین بسترِ بی‌خوابی‌یِ راز
نقشِ رؤیائی‌یِ رُخسارِ تو می‌جویم باز.

با همه چشم تو را می‌جویم
با همه شوق تو را می‌خواهم
زیرِ لب باز تو را می‌خوانم
دائم آهسته به نام

ای مسیحا!
اینک!
مرده‌ئی در دلِ تابوت تکان می‌خورد آرام آرام...

۱۳۳۳
زندانِ قصر

shadows take on color once more
in the mirror's heart,
as a ghost peers through the window
of the dark room,
and from the cold hearth,
a flame leaps from the ashes.

In this sleepless bed of mystery
I trace the contours of your dreamlike face.

    ☐

I search for you with every eye
I call for you in every joy
Under my breath, I call your name
softly and again

O Messiah,

        look!—

a corpse stirs softly in the heart of the coffin…

1954
Qasr prison

عشقِ عمومی

اشک رازی‌ست
لب‌خند رازی‌ست
عشق رازی‌ست

اشکِ آن شب لب‌خندِ عشق‌ام بود.

□

قصه نیستم که بگوئی
نغمه نیستم که بخوانی
صدا نیستم که بشنوی
یا چیزی چنان که ببینی
یا چیزی چنان که بدانی...

من دردِ مشترک‌ام
مرا فریاد کن.

□

درخت با جنگل سخن می‌گوید
علف با صحرا
ستاره با کهکشان
و من با تو سخن می‌گویم

نام‌ات را به من بگو
دست‌ات را به من بده
حرف‌ات را به من بگو
قلب‌ات را به من بده
من ریشه‌هایِ تو را دریافته‌ام
با لبان‌ات برایِ همه لب‌ها سخن گفته‌ام
و دست‌هایی‌ات با دستانِ من آشناست.

در خلوتِ روشن با تو گریسته‌ام
برایِ خاطرِ زنده‌گان،
و در گورستانِ تاریک با تو خوانده‌ام

Common Love

Tears are a mystery
Smiles, a mystery
Love, a mystery

The tears of that night
were the smile of my love.

☐

I am not a tale to be told
not a song to be sung
not a sound to be heard
nor something you can see
or something you can know…

I am common pain—
Cry me out.

☐

The tree speaks with the woods
the weed with the field
the star with the galaxy
and I
speak with you

Tell me your name
give me your hand
tell me your words
give me your heart
I have discovered your depths
and spoken for all through your lips
and your hands are familiar with mine.

I have wept in blazing solitude with you

زیباترین سرودها را
زیرا که مرده‌گانِ این سال
عاشق‌ترینِ زنده‌گان بوده‌اند.

☐

دست‌ات را به من بده
دست‌هایِ تو با من آشناست
ای دیریافته با تو سخن می‌گویم
به‌سانِ ابر که با توفان
به‌سانِ علف که با صحرا
به‌سانِ باران که با دریا
به‌سانِ پرنده که با بهار
به‌سانِ درخت که با جنگل سخن می‌گوید

زیرا که من
ریشه‌هایِ تو را دریافته‌ام
زیرا که صدایِ من
با صدایِ تو آشناست.

۱۳۳۴

for the sake of the living
and sung with you in the darkest of graveyards
the most beautiful of songs
because the dead of this year
were the most loving of the living.

☐

Give me your hand
Your hands know me
O you, found-at-last,
I speak with you
as the cloud with the storm
the weed with the field
the rain with the sea
the bird with the spring
and the tree that speaks with the woods

for I
have discovered your depths
for my voice
is intimate with yours.

1955

بدرود

برای زیستنِ دو قلب لازم است
قلبی که دوست بدارد، قلبی که دوست‌اش بدارند
قلبی که هدیه کند، قلبی که بپذیرد
قلبی که بگوید، قلبی که جواب بگوید
قلبی برایِ من، قلبی برایِ انسانی که من می‌خواهم
تا انسان را در کنارِ خود حس کنم.

◻

دریاهایِ چشمِ تو خشکیدنی‌ست
من چشمه‌ئی زاینده می‌خواهم.

پستان‌هایِ‌ات ستاره‌هایِ کوچک است
آن سویِ ستاره من انسانی می‌خواهم:

انسانی که مرا بگزیند
انسانی که من او را بگزینم،
انسانی که به دست‌هایِ من نگاه کند
انسانی که به دست‌هایِ‌اش نگاه کنم،
انسانی در کنارِ من
تا به دست‌هایِ انسان‌ها نگاه کنیم،
انسانی در کنارَم، آینه‌ئی در کنارم
تا در او بخندم، تا در او بگریم...

◻

خدایان نجات‌ام نمی‌دادند
پیوندِ تُردِ تو نیز
نجات‌ام نداد
نه پیوندِ تُردِ تو
نه چشم‌ها و نه پستان‌هایِ‌ات
نه دست‌هایِ‌ات

کنارِ من قلب‌اَت آینه‌ئی نبود
کنارِ من قلب‌اَت بشری نبود...

۱۳۳۴

Farewell

To exist, you need two hearts:
one heart to love, one heart to be loved
one to give, one to receive
one to call, one to respond
a heart for me, a heart for the one I long for—
to feel someone by my side.

    ☐

The seas in your eye can dry up—
I long for an endless spring.

Your breasts are tiny stars—
beyond the stars, I want someone:

someone who chooses me
and someone I choose
someone who looks at my hands
and lets me see theirs
someone by my side
to see the hands of others together
someone by my side, a mirror by my side
to laugh in, to cry in...

    ☐

The gods didn't save me,
nor did your brittle union—
not your brittle union
                      not your eyes, your breasts,
                                        nor your hands

By my side, your heart was no mirror—
it wasn't even human...

    1955

از عموهای‌ات

برای سیاووشِ کوچک

نه به خاطرِ آفتاب نه به خاطرِ حماسه
به خاطرِ سایه‌ی بامِ کوچک‌اش
به خاطرِ ترانه‌ئی
کوچک‌تر از دست‌هایِ تو

نه به خاطرِ جنگل‌ها نه به خاطرِ دریا
به خاطرِ یک برگ
به خاطرِ یک قطره
روشن‌تر از چشم‌هایِ تو

نه به خاطرِ دیوارها – به خاطرِ یک چپر
نه به خاطرِ همه انسان‌ها – به خاطرِ نوزادِ دشمن‌اش شاید
نه به خاطرِ دنیا – به خاطرِ خانه‌ی تو
به خاطرِ یقینِ کوچک‌ات
که انسان دنیائی‌ست

به خاطرِ آرزویِ یک لحظه‌ی من که پیشِ تو باشم
به خاطرِ دست‌هایِ کوچک‌ات در دست‌هایِ بزرگِ من
و لب‌هایِ بزرگِ من
بر گونه‌هایِ بی‌گناهِ تو

به خاطرِ پرستوئی در باد، هنگامی که تو هلهله می‌کنی
به خاطرِ شب‌نمی بر برگ، هنگامی که تو خفته‌ای
به خاطرِ یک لب‌خند
هنگامی که مرا در کنارِ خود ببینی

به خاطرِ یک سرود
به خاطرِ یک قصه در سردترین شب‌ها تاریک‌ترین شب‌ها
به خاطرِ عروسک‌هایِ تو، نه به خاطرِ انسان‌هایِ بزرگ
به خاطرِ سنگ‌فرشی که مرا به تو می‌رساند، نه به خاطرِ شاه‌راه‌هایِ دوردست

About Your Uncles

For little Siavoosh

Not for the sun's sake, not for the saga's sake
but for the shade from his little rooftop
for the sake of a song
               smaller even than your hands

Not for the woods, not for the sea
but for a single leaf
for a droplet
               brighter even than your eyes

Not for walls, but for a straw hedge
Not for everyone's sake, but maybe for his enemy's newborn
Not for the world, but for your home
for your small conviction
that every human is a world within

For my dream of a moment beside you
for your little hands in my grown-up hands
and my full lips
on your innocent cheeks

For a swallow in the wind when you rejoice
for a dewdrop on a leaf when you sleep
for a single smile
when you see me near

For an anthem
for a story in the coldest of nights, the darkest of nights
for your dolls, not for the grown-ups
for the cobblestones that lead me to you, not for the distant highways

به خاطرِ ناودان، هنگامی که می‌بارد
به خاطرِ کندوها و زنبورهای کوچک
به خاطرِ جارِ سپیدِ ابر در آسمانِ بزرگِ آرام

به خاطرِ تو
به خاطرِ هر چیزِ کوچک هر چیزِ پاک بر خاک افتادند
به یاد آر
عموهای‌ات را می‌گویم
از **مرتضا** سخن می‌گویم.

۱۳۳۴

For the drain pipes when it rains
for the beehives and little bees
for the white herald of the cloud
in the still-open sky

For your sake
for all things pure and small they fell to the earth
Remember them
I am talking about your uncles
I am talking about Morteza.

   1955

باغِ آینه
۱۳۳۹

Garden of Mirrors

1960

حریقِ قلعه‌ئی خاموش...

براىِ مادرم

زنى شب تا سحر گریید خاموش.
زنى شب تا سحر نالید، تا من
سحرگاهى بر آرم دست و گردم
چراغى خُرد و آویزم به برزن.

زنى شب تا سحر نالید و – افسوس! –
مرا آن ناله‌ى خامُش نیفروخت:
حریقِ قلعه‌ى خاموشِ مردم
شب‌اَم دامن گرفت و صبح‌دم سوخت.

حریقِ قلعه‌ى خاموش و مدفون
به خاکستر فرو دهلیز و درگاه
حریقِ قلعه‌ى خاموش – آرى –
نه شب گریِیدنِ زن تا سحرگاه.

۱۹ اسفند ۱۳۳۶

The Flame of a Silent Fort

For my mother

A woman silently wept from dusk to dawn.
She moaned from dusk to dawn
wishing me to rise and become a light
to hang on the people's porch.

A woman moaned from dusk to dawn, but alas,
her silent sobbing didn't rouse me—
the flame of the people's silent fort
set my night ablaze and burned by dawn.

The flame of the silent, sunken fort,
its corridors and gates reduced to cinders—yes
the flame of the silent fort,
not the woman's night-weeping until dawn.

March 10, 1958

باغ آینه

چراغی به دستام چراغی در برابرم.
من به جنگِ سیاهی می‌روم.

گهواره‌هایِ خسته‌گی
از کشاکشِ رفت و آمدها
بازایستاده‌اند،

و خورشیدی از اعماق
کهکشان‌هایِ خاکستر شده را روشن می‌کند.

□

فریادهای عاصی‌یِ آذرخش –
هنگامی که تگرگ
در بطنِ بی‌قرارِ ابر
نطفه می‌بندد.

و دردِ خاموش‌وارِ تاک –
هنگامی که غوره‌یِ خُرد
در انتهایِ شاخ‌سارِ طولانی‌یِ پیچ‌پیچ جوانه می‌زند.

فریادِ من از همه گریز از درد بود
چرا که من در وحشت‌انگیزترینِ شب‌ها آفتاب را به دعائی نومیدوار طلب می‌کرده‌ام.

□

تو از خورشیدها آمده‌ای از سپیده‌دم‌ها آمده‌ای
تو از آینه‌ها و ابریشم‌ها آمده‌ای.

□

در خلئی که نه خدا بود و نه آتش، نگاه و اعتمادِ تو را به دعائی نومیدوار طلب کرده بودم.

جریانی جدی
در فاصله‌یِ دو مرگ
در تهی‌یِ میانِ دو تنهائی –
[نگاه و اعتمادِ تو بدین‌گونه است!]

Garden of Mirrors

A lamp in my hand, a lamp before me,
I go to battle darkness.

The cradles of fatigue
         have stopped rocking,
                 worn out from the tug of the back and forths,
and from the depths, a sun
lights the galaxies turned to ash.

☐

The rebel yells of lightning—
when hail germinates
         in the restless belly of clouds.
The quiet pain of the vine—
as the tiny, unripe grape
         buds at the end of a long, twisting branch.
My cry was always an escape from pain—
a hopeless prayer searching for the sun in the scariest of nights.

☐

You have come from the suns, from the dawns
from mirrors and silk chiffons.

☐

In a godless void without fire, with a desperate prayer, I had reached for
    your gaze and trust.

A solemn current
between two deaths
in the emptiness between two solitudes—
that's what your gaze and trust are!

▫︎
شادی‌یِ تو بی‌رحم است و بزرگ‌وار
نفس‌ات در دست‌هایِ خالی‌یِ من ترانه و سبزی‌ست

من
برمی‌خیزم!

چراغی در دست، چراغی در دل‌ام.
زنگارِ روح‌ام را صیقل می‌زنم.
آینه‌ئی برابرِ آینه‌ات می‌گذارم
تا با تو
ابدیتی بسازم.

۱۵ آذرِ ۱۳۳۶

☐

Your joy is merciless and generous
Your breath in my empty hands is life and song.

I will rise!

A lamp in my hand, a lamp in my heart
I'll polish the rust from my soul,
place a mirror before yours
to build an eternity
               with you.

December 5, 1957

خوابِ وجین‌گر

خواب چون درفکند از پای‌ام
خسته می‌خوابم از آغازِ غروب
لیک آن هرزه علف‌ها که به دست
ریشه‌کن می‌کنم از مزرعه، روز،
می‌کَنَمْشان شب در خواب، هنوز...

۱۳۳۸

The Gardener's Dream

When sleep brings me to my feet
I take to bed at sundown
yet I carry on pulling the same wild weeds
I pull from the field by daylight
even as I sleep at night...

1959

ماهی

من فکر می‌کنم
هرگز نبوده قلبِ من
این‌گونه
گرم و سُرخ:

احساس می‌کنم
در بدترین دقایقِ این شامِ مرگ‌زای
چندین هزار چشمه‌یِ خورشید
در دلم
می‌جوشد از یقین؛
احساس می‌کنم
در هر کنار و گوشه‌یِ این شوره‌زارِ یأس
چندین هزار جنگلِ شاداب
ناگهان
می‌روید از زمین.

□

آه ای یقین گم‌شده، ای ماهی‌یِ گریز
در برکه‌هایِ آینه لغزیده تو به تو!
من آب‌گیرِ صافی‌ام، اینک! به سِحرِ عشق؛
از برکه‌هایِ آینه راهی به من بجو!

□

من فکر می‌کنم
هرگز نبوده
دستِ من
این سان بزرگ و شاد:

احساس می‌کنم
در چشمِ من
به آبشرِ اشکِ سُرخ‌گون
خورشیدِ بی‌غروبِ سرودی کشد نفس؛

Fish

My heart
has never been
        this warm, this red:

Even in the worst moments of this deadly night
thousands of sun-springs well up
        in my heart
from certainty.
In every crevice and corner of this desert of despair
thousands of lush forests
        burst from the earth.

☐

O lost certainty, you runaway fish,
slipping layer by shimmering layer into the mirror pools!
I am a clear pond now—by the spell of love!
Find your way to me through the mirror pools!

☐

My hand
has never been
        this glad, this grand:

A song's never-setting sun
        breathes through the cascade of crimson tears
spilling from my eyes.

Now
in every vein
        to every heartbeat
the waking bells
of a caravan ring.

احساس می‌کنم
در هر رگ‌ام
به هر تپشِ قلبِ من
کنون
بیدارباشِ قافله‌ئی می‌زند جرس.

□

آمد شبی برهنه‌ام از در
چو روحِ آب
در سینه‌اش دو ماهی و در دستَ‌اش آینه
گیسویِ خیسِ او خزه بو، چون خزه به هم.

من بانگ برکشیدم از آستانِ یأس:
«ـ آه ای یقینِ یافته، بازت نمی‌نهم!»

۱۳۳۸

☐

She came to me naked through the door one night,
                                                                               like a water sprite—
two fish at her breast, a mirror in her hand,
her wet hair moss-scented, like moss intertwined.

I screamed at the edge of despair:
O, newfound certainty—I will never let you go again!

    1959

فقر

از رنجی خسته‌ام که از آنِ من نیست
بر خاکی نشسته‌ام که از آنِ من نیست

با نامی زیسته‌ام که از آنِ من نیست
از دردی گریسته‌ام که از آنِ من نیست

از لذتی جان‌گرفته‌ام که از آنِ من نیست
به مرگی جان می‌سپارم که از آنِ من نیست.

۱۳۳۸

Poverty

I'm tired of anguish that isn't mine
I walk an earth that isn't mine

I live with a name that isn't mine
I cry out from pain that isn't mine

I rise with joy that isn't mine
I will die a death that isn't mine

1959

لوحِ گور

نه در رفتن حرکت بود
نه در ماندن سکونی.

شاخه‌ها را از ریشه جدائی نبود
و بادِ سخن‌چین
با برگ‌ها رازی چنان نگفت
که بشاید.

دوشیزه‌یِ عشقِ من مادری بیگانه است
و ستاره‌یِ پُرشتاب
در گذرگاهی مأیوس
بر مداری جاودانه می‌گردد.

۱۳۳۸

Epitaph

There was no motion in leaving,
no peace in staying.

There was no severing of branches from roots,
and the gossiping wind
whispered no secret to the leaves
worth keeping.

The maiden of my love is a distant mother,
and the racing star
orbits
a hopeless loop.

    1959

لحظه‌ها و همیشه
۱۳۴۳

Instants and Eternity

1964

میلاد

نفسِ کوچکِ باد بود و حریرِ نازکِ مهتاب بود و فواره و باغ بود * و شبْ نیمه‌یِ چارمین بود که عروسِ تازه به باغِ مهتاب‌زده فرود آمد از سرا گام‌زنان * اندیش‌ناک از حرارتی تازه که در رگ‌های کبودِ پستان‌اش می‌گذشت * و این خود به تبِ سنگین خاک مانند بود که لیمویِ نارس از آن بهره می‌بَرَد * و در چشم‌های‌اش که به سبزه و مهتاب می‌نگریست نگاهِ شرم بود از احساسِ عطشی نو شناخت که در لُمبرهای‌اش می‌سوخت * و این خود عطشی سیری‌ناپذیر بود چونان ناسیرابی‌یِ جاودانه‌یِ علف، که سرسبزیِ صحرا را مایه به دست می‌دهد * و شرم‌ناکِ خاطره‌ئی لغزان و گریزان و دیربه‌دست بود از آن‌چه با تن او رفت؛ میان او – بیگانه با ماجرا – و بیگانه مردی چنان تند، که با راه‌هایِ تن‌اش آن‌گونه چالاک یگانه بود * و بدان‌گونه آزمند بر اندام خفته‌یِ او دست می‌سود * و جنبش‌اش به نسیمی می‌مانست از بویِ علف‌هایِ آفتاب‌خورده پُر، که پرده‌هایِ شکوفه را به زیر می‌افکَنَد تا دانه‌یِ نارس آشکاره شود.

نفسِ کوچکِ باد بود و حریرِ نازکِ مهتاب بود * و فواره‌یِ باغ بود که با حرکت‌هایِ بازوهایِ نازک‌اش بر آب‌گیر خُرد می‌رقصید *
و عروسِ تازه بر پهنه‌یِ چمن بخفت، در شبْ نیمه‌یِ چارمین *
و در آن دم، من در برگ‌چه‌هایِ نو رُسته بودم * یا در نسیم لغزان * و ای‌بسا که در آب‌هایِ ژرف * و نفسِ بادی که شکوفه‌یِ کوچک را بر درختِ ستبر می‌جنباند در من ناله می‌کرد * و چشمه‌هایِ روشنِ باران در من می‌گریست *

نفسِ کوچکِ باد بود و حریرِ نازکِ مهتاب بود و فواره‌یِ باغ بود * و عروسِ تازه که در شبْ نیمه‌یِ چارمین بر بسترِ علف‌های نورُسته خفته بود با آتشی در نهادش، از احساسِ مردی در کنارِ خویش بر خود بلرزید *
و من برگ و برکه نبودم * نه باد و نه باران * ای روحِ گیاهی! تنِ من زندانِ تو بود *
و عروسِ تازه، پیش از آن که لبانِ پدرم را بر لبانِ خود احساس کند از روحِ درخت و باد و برکه بار گرفت، در شبْ نیمه‌یِ چارمین * و من شهریِ بی‌برگ‌وباد را زندانِ خود کردم بی‌آن‌که خاطره‌یِ باد و برگ از من بُگریزد.

چون زاده شدم چشمان‌ام به دو برگِ نارون می‌مانست، رگان‌ام به ساقه‌یِ نیلوفر، دستان‌ام به پنجه‌یِ افرا * و روحی لغزنده به‌سانِ باد و برکه، به گونه‌یِ باران * و چندان که نارونِ پیر از غضبِ رعد به خاک افتاد دردی جان‌گزا

Genesis

There was the faint breath of wind and the thin silk of moonlight and fountain and garden * And it was on the fourth midnight when the new bride landed from home in the moonstruck garden wandering * pondering the new heat coursing through her breasts' blue veins * itself like the earth's burning fever that feeds unripe lemons * And there was in her eyes that watched the moonlight and flora shame from the newly awakened lust burning in her loins * unquenchable like the ever-insatiable thirst of grass that feeds the meadow's greenness * And she was ashamed of an elusive faltering and fleeting memory of what befell her body, between her—alien to the event—and a fierce alien-man swift and wise with the ways of her body * sweeping so covetous a hand on her sleeping body * moving as a breeze charged with the scent of sun-soaked grass that peels away the blossom-sheaths to reveal the unripe seed

There was the faint breath of wind and the thin silk of moonlight * and the garden's fountain that danced in the little pond with its swaying lithe arms * And on the fourth midnight the new bride slumbered on the stretch of grass * And in the same breath, I was in the newly sprouted leaves * or in the fluttering breeze * and perhaps even in the deep waters * And the breath of the wind stirring little blossoms on the thick tree wailed in me * and bright streams of rain wept in me *

There was the faint breath of wind and the thin silk of moonlight and the garden's fountain * And on the fourth midnight the new bride sleeping on the bed of newly sprouted grass with fire in her core trembled unto herself from sensing a man beside her *

And I was neither leaf nor lake * neither wind nor rain * Oh you Plant Spirit! My body was your prison house * And the new bride was inseminated by the spirit of tree and wind and water before sensing my father's lips upon hers on the fourth midnight * And I turned a leafless and windless city into my prison house without the memory of wind and leaf ever escaping me.

چونان فریادِ مرگ در من شکست *
و من ای طبیعتِ مشقت‌آلوده، ای پدر! فرزندِ تو بودم.

۱۶ اردیبهشتِ ۱۳۳۹

My eyes were like two elm leaves when I was born, my veins like water lily vine, my hands maple claws * my spirit fleeting like wind and water, like rain * And a life-sucking pain like the cry of death burst in me as the old elm fell to the land by the thunder's wrath *
and I, O pain-ridden nature, O father, I was your child.

May 6, 1960

پایتختِ عطش

> آب کم جو. تشنگی آور به دست!
> – ملایِ روم

۱

آفتاب، آتشِ بی‌دریغ است
و رؤیایِ آب‌شاران
در مرزِ هر نگاه.

بر درگاهِ هر ثُقبه
سایه‌ها
  روسبیانِ آرامش‌اند.
پی‌جویِ آن سایه‌یِ بزرگام من که عطشِ خشک‌دشت را باطل می‌کند.

□

چه پگاه و چه پسین،
این‌جا
  نیم‌روز
    مظهرِ «هست» است:
آتشِ سوزنده را رنگی و اعتباری نیست
دروازه‌یِ امکان بر باران بسته است
شن از حُرمتِ رود و بسترِ شن‌پوشِ خشک‌رود از وحشتِ «هرگز» سخن می‌گوید.
بوته‌یِ گز به عبث سایه‌ئی در خلوتِ خویش می‌جوید.

□

ای شبِ تشنه! خدا کجاست؟
تو
  روزِ دیگرگونه‌ای
    به رنگی دیگر
که با تو
  در آفرینشِ تو
    بی‌دادی رفته است:
تو زنگی‌یِ زمانی.

The Capital of Thirst

> *Seldom seek water. Find thirst instead!*
> —Rumi

1

The sun is fire unbound,
and waterfalls a dream
at the edge of every gaze.

At the threshold of every pupil,
shadows—
        courtesans of comfort.
I seek that great shade to quench the thirst of sun-baked fields.

☐

Be it dawn or dusk,
here
    midday
            is the essence of being:
The blazing fire has lost color and quality
The portals of the possible stay closed to the rain
The sand speaks of the river's sanctity while the sand-covered riverbed
    speaks of its fear of never
In vain, the lone thornbush seeks shade.

☐

O thirsty night! Where is God?
You
    are day disguised
            in another shade
because there was cruelty
            in creating you:
you are the black tar of time.

۲

کنارِ تو را ترک گفته‌ام
و زیرِ این آسمانِ نگون‌سار که از جنبشِ هر پرنده تهی‌ست و هلالی کدر چونان
مُرده‌ماهی‌یِ سیم‌گونه فلسی بر سطحِ بی‌موجاش می‌گذرد
به بازجُستِ تو برخاسته‌ام
تا در پایتختِ عطش
در جلوه‌ئی دیگر
بازت یابم.

ای آبِ روشن!
تو را با معیارِ عطش می‌سنجم.

□

در این سرابچه
آیا
زورقِ تشنه‌گی‌ست
آن‌چه مرا به‌سویِ شما می‌راند
یا خود
زمزمه‌یِ شماست
و من نه به خود می‌روم
که زمزمه‌یِ شما
به جانبِ خویش‌ام می‌خواند؟

نخلِ من ای واحه‌ی من!
در پناهِ شما چشمه‌سارِ خنکی هست
که خاطره‌اش
عُریان‌ام می‌کند.

۱۸ خردادِ ۱۳۳۹
چابهار

2

I have left your side
under this cursed sky, where no birds fly, where a crescent moon,
dull as a lifeless fish with silver scales, drifts across its waveless plain,
and I have risen to find you
                      once more
with a new face
in the capital of thirst.

Oh clear water!
I measure you with the scale of thirst.

☐

In this little mirage
is it
the raft of thirst
                that draws me toward you
or is it
      your whisper?
I go—not by my own will—
                      but because your whisper calls me.

My palm tree, my oasis!
In your refuge lies a cool spring
whose memory
undresses me.

    June 8, 1960
    Chabahar

میانِ ماندن و رفتن...

میانِ ماندن و رفتن حکایتی کردیم
که آشکارا در پرده‌ی کنایت رفت.
مجالِ ما همه این تنگ‌مایه بود و، دریغ
که مایه خود همه در وجهِ این حکایت رفت.

۲۸ خردادِ ۱۳۳۹

Between Staying and Going...

Between staying and going we made up a story
veiled in obvious irony.
The little we had
was squandered on this story.

June 18, 1960

حماسه!

در چارراه‌ها خبری نیست:
یک عده می‌روند
یک عده خسته بازمی‌آیند

و انسان – که کهنه‌رند خدائی‌ست بی‌گمان –
بی‌شوق و بی‌امید
برایِ دو قرصِ نان
کاپوت می‌فروشد
در معبرِ زمان.

□

در کوچه
پُشتِ قوطی‌یِ سیگار
شاعری
اِستاد و بالبداهه نوشت این حماسه را:
«– انسان، خداست.
حرفِ من این است.
گر کفر یا حقیقتِ محض است این سخن،
انسان خداست.
آری. این است حرفِ من!»

. . . .

از بوقِ یک دوچرخه‌سوارِ الاغِ پست
شاعر ز جای جَست و...
... مدادش، نوکاش شکست!

۲۸ آذرِ ۱۳۳۹

Epic!

Nothing's happening at the intersection:
Some people cut through,
others come back beat.

And then there's a tired old hustler, a holy trickster,
lost and grim,
        who's dealing condoms
for two loaves of bread
        on the highway of time.

   ☐

Down the alley
        a poet stops
                and on the back of a cigarette case
improvises this epic:
   Humans are gods
   That's what I'm saying
   Blasphemy or fact
   Humans are gods
   Yes, that's what I'm saying!

. . . .

All of a sudden—
HORN—
a dimwit fool on a bike zips by
The poet jumps and
        snap,
            his pencil tip breaks!

   December 19, 1960

کوه‌ها

کوه‌ها با هم‌اند و تنهای‌اند
هم‌چو ما، با همانِ تنهایان.

۱۳۳۹

The Mountains

The mountains are together and alone
Like us, the together-alones.

1960

انگیزه‌هایِ خاموشی

پس آدم، ابوالبشر، به پیرامنِ خویش نظاره کرد * و بر زمینِ عُریان نظاره کرد * و به آفتاب که روی درمی‌پوشید نظاره کرد * و در این هنگام، بادهایِ سرد بر خاکِ برهنه می‌جنبید * و سایه‌ها همه‌جا بر خاک می‌جنبید * و هر چیز دیدنی به هیأتِ سایه‌ئی درآمده در سایه‌یِ عظیم می‌خلید * و روحِ تاریکی بر قالبِ خاک منتشر بود * و هر چیز بِسودنی دست‌مایه‌یِ وهمیِ دیگرگونه بود * و آدم، ابوالبشر، به جُفتِ خویش درنگریست * و او در چشم‌های جُفتِ خویش نظر کرد که در آن ترس و سایه بود * و در خاموشی در او نظر کرد * و تاریکی در جانِ او نشست.

و این نخستین بار بود، بر زمین و در همه آسمان، که گفتنی سخنی ناگفته ماند *

پس چون **هابیل** به قفای خویش نظر کرد **قابیل** را بدید * و او را چون رعدِ آسمان‌ها خروشان یافت * و او را چون آبِ رودخانه پیچان یافت * و برادرِ خون‌اش را به‌سانِ سنگِ کوه سرد و سخت یافت * و او را دریافت * و او را با بداندیشی همراه یافت، چون ماده میشی که نوزادش در قفای اوست * و او را چون مرغانِ نخجیر با چنگالِ گشوده دید * و برادرِ خون‌اش را به خونِ خویش آزمند یافت * و **قابیل** در برادرِ خونِ خویش نظر کرد * و در چشمِ او شگفتی و ناباوری بود * و در خاموشی به جانبِ **هابیل** نظر کرد * و آئینه‌یِ مهتاب‌ها در جان‌اش با شاخه‌ی نازکِ رگ‌های‌اش شکست.

و این خود بارِ نخستین نبود، بر زمین و در همه‌یِ زمین، که گفتنی‌سخنی بر لبی ناگفته می‌ماند.

و از آن پس، بسیارها گفتنی هست که ناگفته می‌ماند * چون ما – تو و من – به هنگامِ دیدارِ نخستین * که نگاهِ ما به هم درایستاد، و گفتنی‌ها به خاموشی در نشست * و از آن پس چه بسیار گفتنی هست که ناگفته می‌ماند بر لبِ آدمیان * بدان هنگام که کبوترِ آشتی بر بامِ ایشان می‌نشیند * به هنگامِ اعتراف و به گاهِ وصل * به هنگامِ وداع و – از آن بیش – بدان هنگام که بازمی‌گردند تا به قفایِ خویش درنگرند...

و از آن پس، گفتنی‌ها، تا ناگفته بمانَد انگیزه‌هایِ بسیار یافت.

۱۵ اسفندِ ۱۳۳۹

Reasons for Silence

Then Adam, the first human, looked around him * and studied the barren earth * watching as the sun concealed its face * In that moment, cold winds swept over the naked soil * shadows moved across the land * and all that was visible became a shadow within a great shadow * The spirit of darkness imprinted itself upon the earth * and everything tangible became the source of another illusion * Adam, the first human, looked at his mate * and saw fear and shadow in her eyes * Silently, he gazed at her * and darkness settled within his soul.

And this was the first time on earth and all of the heavens that words meant to be spoken remained unspoken *

Then Abel looked behind him and saw Cain * roaring like the thunder of heavens * twisted like river water * a blood brother cold and hard like mountain rock * and Abel understood him * and found his blood brother harboring malevolence, like a mother ewe with her lamb trailing behind her * like a bird of prey with open claws * a blood brother greedy for his blood * and Cain looked at his blood brother * whose eyes were filled with astonishment and disbelief * In silence, he turned toward Abel * and within him shattered the mirror of moonlight, as did the delicate branches of his veins.

And this was not the first time on earth and across the lands that words meant to be spoken remained unspoken on silent lips.

Since then, many words meant to be spoken have remained unspoken * like with us—you and me—at our first encounter * when our eyes met and words settled into silence * Since then, many words meant to be spoken have remained unspoken on the people's lips: * when the dove of peace perches on their roof * during moments of confession and union * in farewells, and—even more so—when they turn to look behind them...

And since then, words meant to be spoken have found many reasons to remain unspoken.

March 6, 1961

غزلِ ناتمام...

به هر تارِ جان‌ام صد آواز هست
دریغا که دستی به مضراب نیست.
چو رؤیا به حسرت گذشتم، که شب
فرو خفت و با کس سرِ خواب نیست.
. . . .

۱۳۳۹

Unfinished Ghazal

For each string of my soul, a hundred songs
No hand holds the pick.
Like a dream I lived in longing, because night
faded and no one shared it with me.
. . . .

1960

شبانه (آن‌که دانست)

> وان را که خبر شد، خبری باز نیامد
> – سعدی

آن‌که دانست، زبان بست
وان که می‌گفت، ندانست...

☐

چه غم‌آلوده شبی بود!
وان مسافر که در آن ظلمتِ خاموش گذشت
و بر انگیخت سگان را به صدایِ سُمِ اسب‌اش بر سنگ
بی‌که یک دَم به خیال‌اش گذرد
که فرود آید شب را،
گوئی
همه رؤیایِ تبی بود.

چه غم‌آلوده شبی بود!

آذرِ ۱۳۴۰

Nocturnal (He Who Knew)

> *And he who was awakened was never heard from again*
> —Sa'di

He who knew, held his tongue
and he who spoke, did not know...

□

What a sorrow-filled night it was!
The traveler crossing that silent night,
provoking dogs with the clatter of his horse's hooves on stone,
never once pausing to consider
dismounting for the night,
seemed nothing more than a fever dream.

What a sorrow-filled night it was!

December 1961

من مرگ را...

اینک موجِ سنگین‌گذرِ زمان است که در من می‌گذرد.
اینک موجِ سنگین‌گذرِ زمان است که چون جوبارِ آهن در من می‌گذرد.
اینک موجِ سنگین‌گذرِ زمان است که چونان دریائی از پولاد و سنگ در من می‌گذرد.

□

در گذرگاهِ نسیم سرودی دیگرگونه آغاز کردم
در گذرگاهِ باران سرودی دیگرگونه آغاز کردم
در گذرگاهِ سایه سرودی دیگرگونه آغاز کردم.

نیلوفر و باران در تو بود
خنجر و فریادی در من،
فواره و رؤیا در تو بود
تالاب و سیاهی در من.

در گذرگاهاتِ سرودی دیگرگونه آغاز کردم.

□

من برگ را سرودی کردم
سر سبزتر زِ بیشه

من موج را سرودی کردم
پُرنبض‌تر زِ انسان

من عشق را سرودی کردم
پُرطبل‌تر زِ مرگ

سر سبزتر زِ جنگل
من برگ را سرودی کردم

پُرتپش‌تر از دلِ دریا
من موج را سرودی کردم

I…Death

Now the heavy tide of time courses through me.
Now the heavy tide of time courses through me like a river of iron.
Now the heavy tide of time courses through me like a sea of steel
    and stone.

    ☐

I sang a new song, crossing the breeze
I sang a new song, crossing the rain
I sang a new song, crossing the shadow.

In you, water lily and rain,
In me, dagger and scream
In you, fountain and dream,
In me, swamp and shadow.

I sang a new song, crossing your path.

    ☐

I turned a leaf into a song
greener than the grove

I turned a wave into a song
livelier than people

I turned love into a song
louder than death

Greener than the forest—
I turned a leaf into a song

Beating harder than the sea's heart—
I turned a wave into a song

پُرطبل‌تر از حیات
من مرگ را
سرودی کردم.

آذرِ ۱۳۴۰

Louder than life,
I turned death
into a song.

December 1961

شبانه (کوچه‌ها باریکن)

به گوهرِ مراد

کوچه‌ها باریکن
دُکّونا
بسته‌س،
خونه‌ها تاریکن
تاقا
شیکسته‌س،
از صدا
افتاده
تار و کمونچه
مُرده می‌برن
کوچه به
کوچه.

□

نگا کن!
مُرده‌ها
به مُرده
نمی‌رن،
حتا به
شمعِ جون سپرده
نمی‌رن،
شکلِ
فانوسی‌یَن
که اگه خاموشه
واسه نَف نیس
هَنو
یه عالم نَف توشه.

Nocturnal (The Alleys are Tight)

To Gohar-e Morad

The alleys are tight
        Corner stores
                shut down
Houses
      dark
          Roofs
              cracked
No music
        from the tar
                and the kamancheh
Alley
    to alley
        they carry
            the dead.

☐

Look!
    The dead
        don't even look
                like the dead
    Not even like
        candles
            just snuffed out
They're like lamps
        that quit
                but not 'cause the oil's gone—
there's still
        plenty left.

◻

جماعت!
من دیگه
حوصله
ندارم
به «خوب»
امید و
از «بد» گله
ندارم.

گرچه از
دیگرون
فاصله
ندارم،
کاری با
کارِ این
قافله
ندارم!

◻

کوچه‌ها
باریکن
دُکّونا
بسته‌س،
خونه‌ها
تاریکن
تاقا
شیکسته‌س،
از صدا
افتاده
تار و
کمونچه
مُرده
می‌برن
کوچه به
کوچه...

۱۳۴۰

☐

    Listen up, people!
              I'm done
                      I've got no more
                                patience
  No more hope
          for the "good"
                  or gripes
                            about the "bad."
  Even though
            I'm around
  I want
          nothing
                  to do
                          with this crowd!

☐

    The alleys are tight
                  Corner stores
                              shut down
  Houses
        dark
            Roofs
                  cracked
  No music
          from the tar
                          and the kamancheh
  Alley
      to alley
            they carry
                    the dead…

1961

آیدا در آینه
۱۳۴۳

Aida in the Mirror

1964

آغاز

بی‌گاهان
به غربت
به زمانی که خود در نرسیده بود –

چنین زاده شدم در بیشه‌ی جانوران و سنگ،
و قلبام
در خلأ
تپیدن آغاز کرد.

□

گهواره‌ی تکرار را ترک گفتم
در سرزمینی بی‌پرنده و بی‌بهار.

نخستین سفرم بازآمدن بود از چشم‌اندازهای امیدفرسای ماسه و خار،
بی آن‌که با نخستین قدم‌هایِ ناآزموده‌یِ نوپائی‌یِ خویش به راهی دور رفته باشم.

نخستین سفرم
بازآمدن بود.

□

دوردست
امیدی نمی‌آموخت.
لرزان
بر پاهایِ نو راه
رو در افقِ سوزان ایستادم.
دریافتم که بشارتی نیست
چرا که سرابی در میانه بود.

□

دوردست امیدی نمی‌آموخت.
دانستم که بشارتی نیست:
این بی‌کرانه
زندانی چندان عظیم بود

The Beginning

Beyond time
in unknown lands
at a moment yet to come—

this is how I was born in a thicket of beasts and stones,
and in the void
my heart
began to beat.

☐

I left the cradle of repetition
in a land without birds or spring.

My first journey was a retreat from the dispiriting sights of sand and
    thorns, never having
ventured far on the untrained steps of my youth.

My first journey
was a retreat.

☐

The distant horizon
offered no hope.
Shaking
        on untravelled legs,
                I stood before a burning horizon,
realizing there was no promise
because a mirage stood in the way.

☐

The distant horizon offered no hope.
I understood there was no promise:
this vast expanse

که روح

از شرمِ ناتوانی
در اشک
پنهان می‌شد.

فروردینِ ۱۳۴۰

       was a prison so immense
                              that the spirit,
ashamed of its frailty
hid
      behind tears.

       April 1961

شبانه (میانِ خورشیدهایِ همیشه)

میانِ خورشیدهایِ همیشه
زیبائی‌یِ تو
لنگری‌ست –
خورشیدی که
از سپیده‌دمِ همه ستاره‌گان
بی‌نیازم می‌کند.

نگاه‌ات
شکستِ ستم‌گری‌ست –
نگاهی که عریانی‌یِ روحِ مرا
از مِهر
جامه‌ئی کرد

بدان‌سان که کنون‌ام
شبِ بی‌روزنِ هرگز
چنان نماید که کنایتی طنزآلود بوده است.

و چشمان‌ات با من گفتند
که فردا
روزِ دیگری‌ست –
آنک چشمانی که خمیرْمایه‌یِ مِهر است!
وینک مِهرِ تو:
نبردْافزاری
تا با تقدیرِ خویش پنجه در پنجه کنم.

□

آفتاب را در فراسوهایِ افق پنداشته بودم.
به جز عزیمتِ نا به هَنگام‌ام گزیری نبود
چنین انگاشته بودم.

آیدا فسخِ عزیمتِ جاودانه بود.

□

Nocturnal (Among the Eternal Suns)

Among the eternal suns
your beauty
is an anchor—
a sun
      that frees me
             from the dawn of all stars.

Your gaze
   is the fall of tyranny—
a gaze that dressed
        my bare soul
            in love
so fully that now
        the darkest night of never
feels like nothing but a comedy of ironies.

Your eyes told me
tomorrow
     is a new day—
eyes that spark love!
And now, your love:
a weapon
     to wrestle with my fate.

   ☐

I had thought the sun lay beyond the horizon,
that no escape remained but an early exit,
or so I had believed.

Then came Aida, undoing the eternal exit.

   ☐

میانِ آفتاب‌هایِ همیشه
زیبائی‌یِ تو
لنگری‌ست –
نگاهات
شکستِ ستم‌گری‌ست –
و چشمان‌ات با من گفتند
که فردا
روزِ دیگری‌ست.

شهریورِ ۱۳۴۱

Among the eternal suns
your beauty
is an anchor—
your gaze
        the fall of tyranny—
and your eyes told me
tomorrow
is a new day.

August 1962

من و تو، درخت و بارون...

من باهارم تو زمین
من زمین‌ام تو درخت
من درخت‌ام تو باهار –
نازِ انگشتایِ بارونِ تو باغ‌ام می‌کنه
میونِ جنگلا تاق‌ام می‌کنه.

تو بزرگی مثِ شب.
اگه مهتاب باشه یا نه
    تو بزرگی
        مثِ شب.

خودِ مهتابی تو اصلاً، خودِ مهتابی تو.
تازه، وقتی بره مهتاب و
    هنوز
      شبِ تنها
    باید
راهِ دوری رو بره تا دَمِ دروازه‌یِ روز –
مثِ شب گود و بزرگی
    مثِ شب.

تازه، روزم که بیاد
    تو تمیزی
      مثِ شبنم
        مثِ صبح.

تو مثِ مخملِ ابری
    مثِ بویِ علفی
    مثِ اون ململِ مه نازکی:
    اون ململِ مه
که رو عطرِ علفا، مثلِ بلاتکلیفی
هاج و واج مونده مردد
    میونِ موندن و رفتن
میونِ مرگ و حیات.

You and Me, the Rain and the Tree

I'm the spring, you're the earth
I'm the earth, you're the tree
I'm the tree, you're the spring—
the touch of your rain-fingers makes me bloom,
crowns me king among the forests in bloom.

You're vast like the night.
Moonlight or not
              you're still vast
                            like the night.

You're the moonlight itself, truly,
the moonlight itself.
Truth is, even when moonlight fades
and the lonely night
must still travel far to reach the gates of dawn—
you're vast,
deep like the night
just like the night.

In fact, even when day comes
you're fresh
              like dew
                    like morning.

You're like velvet clouds
                    the scent of grass
fine like that muslin of mist—
                        that muslin of mist
hanging over the scent of grass like uncertainty,
stunned and unsure
              whether to stay or go,
                        to die or live.

مثِ برفایی تو.
تازه آبم که بشن برفا و عُریون بشه کوه
مثِ اون قله‌یِ مغرورِ بلندی
که به ابرایِ سیاهی و به بادایِ بدی می‌خندی...

□

من باهارم تو زمین
من زمین‌ام تو درخت
من درخت‌ام تو باهار،
نازِ انگشتایِ بارونِ تو باغ‌ام می‌کنه
میونِ جنگلا تاق‌ام می‌کنه.

مهرِ ۱۳۴۱

You're like the snow.
Even if it all melts, leaving the mountains bare,
you're the tall, proud peak
laughing at the dark clouds and the harsh winds...

□

I'm the spring, you're the earth
I'm the earth, you're the tree
I'm the tree, you're the spring—
the touch of your rain-fingers makes me bloom
crowns me king among the forests in bloom.

October 1962

من و تو...

من و تو یکی دهان‌ایم
که با همه آوازش
به زیباتر سرودی خواناست.

من و تو یکی دیدگان‌ایم
که دنیا را هر دَم
در منظرِ خویش
تازه‌تر می‌سازد.

نفرتی
از هرآن‌چه بازمان دارد
از هرآن‌چه محصورِمان کند
از هرآن‌چه وادارِدِمان
که به دنبال بنگریم، ‌–

دستی
که خطی گستاخ به باطل می‌کشد.

□

من و تو یکی شوریم
از هر شعله‌ئی برتر،
که هیچ‌گاه شکست را بر ما چیره‌گی نیست
چرا که از عشق
روئینه‌تن‌ایم.

□

و پرستوئی که در سرْپناهِ ما آشیان کرده است
با آمد شدنی شتاب‌ناک
خانه را
از خدائی گم‌شده
لب‌ریز می‌کند.

۲۳ دیِ ۱۳۴۱

You and I...

You and I are one mouth,
singing with all its voice
a song of beauty.

You and I are one gaze
renewing the world
                each moment
                              in our vision.

A hatred
for all that hinders us
for all that limits us
for all that forces us
                to look back,

a hand
that boldly strikes through falsehood.

☐

You and I are one passion
greater than any flame,
untouched by defeat,
made invincible
by love.

☐

And a swallow nesting in our home
with its swift, darting flights
fills the house
                to the brim
                          with a lost god.

January 13, 1963

از مرگ...

هرگز از مرگ نهراسیده‌ام
اگرچه دستان‌اش از ابتذال شکننده‌تر بود.
هراسِ من ـ باری ـ همه از مردن در سرزمینی‌ست
که مزدِ گورکن
از بهای آزادیِ آدمی
افزون باشد.

□

جُستن
یافتن
و آن‌گاه
به اختیار برگزیدن
و از خویشتن خویش
بارویی پی‌افکندن ـ

اگر مرگ را از این همه ارزشی بیش‌تر باشد
حاشا حاشا که هرگز از مرگ هراسیده باشم.

دیِ ۱۳۴۱

...Death

I've never feared death,
even if its grip were more crushing than the banal.
What I fear—truly fear—is dying in a place
where a gravedigger's pay
                      outweighs
                                  the worth of human freedom.

☐

To seek
to find
and then to freely choose
to build
a fortress
of your own self—

If death is prized above all this,
then heaven forbid I should ever fear death.

January 1963

سرودِ آشنائی

کیستی که من
این‌گونه
به اعتماد

نامِ خود را
با تو می‌گویم
کلیدِ خانه‌ام را
در دست‌ات می‌گذارم
نانِ شادی‌های‌ام را
با تو قسمت می‌کنم
به کنارت می‌نشینم و
بر زانویِ تو

این‌چنین آرام
به خواب می‌روم؟

□

کیستی که من
این‌گونه به جد
در دیارِ رؤیاهای خویش
با تو درنگ می‌کنم؟

۲۹ اردیبهشتِ ۱۳۴۲

Song of Our Meeting

Who are you, that I
               so trustingly
speak
my name to you,
hand
the keys of my home to you,
share
the bread of my joy with you,
sit
alongside you and
sleep
    so peacefully
at your knees?

    ☐

Who are you, that I
               so solemnly
linger with you
in the country
of my dreams?

    May 19, 1963

سرود برایِ سپاس و پرستش

بوسه‌هایِ تو
گنجشککانِ پُرگویِ باغ‌اند
و پستان‌های‌ات کندویِ کوهستان‌هاست
و تن‌ات
رازی‌ست جاودانه
که در خلوتی عظیم
با من‌اش در میان می‌گذارند.

تنِ تو آهنگی‌ست
و تَنِ من کلمه‌ئی که در آن می‌نشیند
تا نغَمه‌ئی در وجود آید:
سرودی که **تداوم** را می‌تپد.

در نگاهات همه‌ی مهربانی‌هاست:
قاصدی که **زندهگی** را خبر می‌دهد.

و در سکوت‌ات همه‌ی صداها:
فریادی که **بودن** را تجربه می‌کند.

۳۱ اردیبهشتِ ۱۳۴۲

Song of Praise and Worship

Your kisses—
chatting little sparrows in the garden
your breasts—
mountain hives
your body—
a timeless mystery
                        we share in sacred solitude.

Your body is a melody,
mine, a word resting in it
to birth a song—
a hymn pulsing with eternity.

Your eyes brim with kindness:
messengers of life itself.

And in your silence, every sound:
a cry that touches existence.

May 21, 1963

آیدا در آینه

لبان‌ات
به ظرافتِ شعر
شهوانی‌ترین بوسه‌ها را به شرمی چنان مبدل می‌کند
که جاندارِ غارنشین از آن سود می‌جوید
تا به صورتِ انسان درآید.

و گونه‌های‌ات
با دو شیارِ مورّب،
که غرورِ تو را هدایت می‌کنند و
سرنوشتِ مرا
که شب را تحمل کرده‌ام
بی‌آن‌که به انتظارِ صبح
مسلح بوده باشم،
و بکارتی سربلند را
از روسبی‌خانه‌های دادوستد
سربه مُهر بازآورده‌ام.

هرگز کسی این‌گونه فجیع به کشتنِ خود برنخاست که من به زنده‌گی نشستم!

□

و چشمان‌ات رازِ آتش است.

و عشق‌ات پیروزی‌یِ آدمی‌ست
هنگامی که به جنگِ تقدیر می‌شتابد.

و آغوش‌ات
اندک جائی برایِ زیستن
اندک جائی برایِ مردن
و گریزِ از شهر
که با هزار انگشت
به وقاحت
پاکی‌یِ آسمان را متهم می‌کند.

Aida in the Mirror

Your lips,
    tender as a poem,
turn the most carnal kisses into innocence so pure
they could make a caveman human.

Your cheeks,
            two slant lines
steering your pride
                    and my fate.
I, who braved the night—
defenseless, waiting for dawn—
retrieved from the brothels of trade
a noble virginity
untouched.

No one ever fought harder to destroy themselves as I have fought to live!

  □

Your eyes hold the secret of fire.

Your love is the triumph of humankind
charging into battle with fate.

Your embrace,
a close shelter to live in,
a place to die in,
an escape from the city
                    that with a thousand shameless fingers
condemns the sky's purity.

☐

کوه با نخستین سنگ‌ها آغاز می‌شود
و انسان با نخستین درد.

در من زندانی‌یِ ستم‌گری بود
که به آوازِ زنجیرش خو نمی‌کرد —
من با نخستین نگاهِ تو آغاز شدم.

☐

توفان‌ها
در رقصِ عظیمِ تو
به شکوه‌مندی
نی‌لبکی می‌نوازند،

و ترانه‌ی رگ‌های‌ات
آفتابِ همیشه را طالع می‌کند.

بگذار چنان از خواب برآیم
که کوچه‌هایِ شهر
حضورِ مرا دریابند.

دستان‌ات آشتی است
و دوستانی که یاری می‌دهند
تا دشمنی
از یاد
برده شود.

پیشانی‌ات آینه‌ئی بلند است
تاب‌ناک و بلند،
که خواهرانِ هفت‌گانه در آن می‌نگرند
تا به زیبایی‌یِ خویش دست یابند.

دو پرنده‌یِ بی‌طاقت در سینه‌هات آواز می‌خوانند.
تابستان از کدامین راه فرا خواهد رسید
تا عطش
آب‌ها را گواراتر کند؟

☐

Mountains are born of the first stone,
humans of the first pain.

In me lived a cruel prisoner
long deaf to the sound of his chains—
until your first glance brought me to life.

☐

Tempests
        play their majestic tune
                on a reed flute
                        in your grand dance,
while the song of your veins
summons the eternal sun.

Let me rise
so the city streets
feel my presence.

Your hands—
a gesture of peace,
friends that help me
        forget enmity.

Your brow—
a high, radiant mirror
where the Seven Sisters
reach their beauty.

Two restless birds sing in your chest.
Which path will summer take
to sweeten our thirst?

تا در آئینه پدیدار آئی
عمری دراز در آن نگریستم
من برکه‌ها و دریاها را گریستم
ای پری‌وارِ در قالبِ آدمی
که پیکرت جز در خُلوارهی ناراستی نمی‌سوزد! ـ
حضورت بهشتی‌ست
که گریز از جهنم را توجیه می‌کند،
دریائی که مرا در خود غرق می‌کند
تا از همه گناهان و دروغ
شسته شوم.

و سپیده‌دم با دست‌های‌ات بیدار می‌شود.

بهمنِ ۱۳۴۲

Waiting for you to appear,
I stared into the mirror for a lifetime,
weeping pools and oceans.
O, fairy-like creature in human form,
whose body burns only in the flames of falsehood!
Your presence is paradise
justifying the flight from hell,
a sea that swallows me whole
to wash away my sins and lies.

And dawn awakens in your hands.

February 1964

میعاد

در فراسویِ مرزهایِ تن‌ات تو را دوست می‌دارم.

آینه‌ها و شب‌پره‌هایِ مشتاق را به من بده
روشنی و شراب را
آسمانِ بلند و کمانِ گشاده‌ی پُل
پرنده‌ها و قوس و قزح را به من بده
و راهِ آخرین را
در پرده‌ئی که می‌زنی مکرر کن.

□

در فراسویِ مرزهایِ تن‌ام
تو را دوست می‌دارم.
در آن دوردستِ بعید
که رسالتِ اندام‌ها پایان می‌پذیرد
و شعله و شورِ تپش‌ها و خواهش‌ها
به تمامی
فرو می‌نشیند
و هر معنا قالبِ لفظ را وامی‌گذارد
چنان چون روحی
که جسد را در پایانِ سفر،
تا به هجومِ کرکس‌هایِ پایان‌اش وانهد...

□

در فراسوهایِ عشق
تو را دوست می‌دارم،
در فراسوهایِ پرده و رنگ.

در فراسوهایِ پیکرهای‌مان
با من وعده‌یِ دیداری بده.

اردیبهشتِ ۱۳۴۳
شیرگاه

Tryst

Beyond the borders of your body, I love you.

Give me mirrors and eager moths,
light and wine,
the high sky and the wide arch of the bridge
Give me birds and rainbows
and keep playing that last melody
in your scale.

☐

Beyond the borders of my body,
I love you—
in that distant beyond
where the body's call fades
where every last flicker of fire, pulse, and longing
                                ebbs into nothingness,
where meaning sheds its words
like a spirit
        leaving the corpse to vultures
in the final hour...

☐

Beyond the limits of love,
I love you—
beyond veils and colors.

Beyond the limits of our bodies
promise me a tryst.

    May 1964
    Shirgah

آیدا:
درخت و خنجر و خاطره!
۱۳۴۴

Aida:
Tree and Dagger and Memory!
1965

شبانه (ما شکیبا بودیم)

ما شکیبا بودیم.
و این است آن کلامی که ما را به تمامی
وصف می‌تواند کرد...

ما شکیبا بودیم.
به شکیبائی‌یِ بشکه‌ئی بر گذرگاهی نهاده؛
که نظاره می‌کند با سکوتی دردانگیز
خالی شدنِ سطل‌هایِ زباله را در انباره‌یِ خویش
و انباشته شدن را
از انگیزه‌هایِ مبتذلِ شادی‌یِ گربه‌گان و سگانِ بی‌صاحبِ کوی،
و پوزه‌یِ ره‌گذاران را
که چون از کنارش می‌گذرند
به شتاب
در دست‌مال‌هائی از درون و برونِ بشکه پلشت‌تر
پنهان می‌شود.

▫

ای محتضران
که امیدی وقیح
خون به رگ‌هاتان می‌گرداند!
من از زوال سخن نمی‌گویم
[یا خود از شما – که فتح زوال‌اید
و وحشت‌هایِ قرنی چنین آلوده‌یِ نامرادی و نامردی را
آن‌گونه به دنبال می‌کشید
که ماده‌سگی
بویِ تندِ ماچه‌گی‌اش را.] –
من از آن امیدِ بی‌هوده سخن می‌گویم
که مرگِ نجات‌بخشِ شما را
به امروز و فردا می‌افکَنَد:
«– مسافری که به انتظار و امیدش نشسته‌اید
از کجا که هم از نیمه‌یِ راه
بازنگشته باشد؟»

۶ شهریورِ ۱۳۴۳

Nocturnal (We Were Patient)

We were patient—
that's the best word for us...

Patient,
like a dumpster by the roadside,
silent and aching,
as garbage bins dump their filth into its depths.
Patient,
as stray cats and dogs scavenge for cheap thrills,
while passersby hurry past,
hiding their snouts
behind handkerchiefs
stained worse—inside and out—
than the dumpster itself.

☐

O dying ones,
                obscene hope
                              pumping blood through your veins!
I'm not talking about demise—
or you, the definition of it,
dragging the horrors of a century,
scarred by cowardice and calamity,
like a she-dog
trailing the sharp scent of her own heat—

I'm talking about that pointless hope
that keeps pushing your redemptive end
                        to some tomorrow and another after that:
    Who's to say the traveler you wait for
    hasn't already turned back halfway?

    August 28, 1964

شبانه (اندکی بدی در نهادِ تو)

اندکی بدی در نهادِ تو
اندکی بدی در نهادِ من
اندکی بدی در نهادِ ما... ‑

و لعنتِ جاودانه بر تبارِ انسان فرود می‌آید.

آب‌ریزی کوچک به هر سراچه ‑ هر چند که خلوتگاهِ عشقی باشد ‑
شهر را
از برایِ آن‌که به گنداب در نشیند
کفایت است.

۶ شهریورِ ۱۳۴۳

Nocturnal (A Bit of Evil in Your Soul)

A bit of evil in your soul
A bit in mine
A bit in us all...

—and the eternal curse befalls humankind.

A tiny latrine in every home, even in the sanctuary of love,
is enough to drag
                an entire city
                              into filth.

August 28, 1964

...و تباهی آغاز یافت

پس پای‌ها استوارتر بر زمین بداشت * تیره‌ی پُشت راست کرد * گردن به غرور برافراشت * و فریاد برداشت: اینک من! آدمی! پادشاهِ زمین!

و جانداران همه از غریو او بهراسیدند * و غروری که خود به غُرّشِ او پنهان بود بر جانداران همه چیره شد * و آدمی جانوران را همه در راه نهاد * و از ایشان برگذشت * و بر ایشان سَر شد از آن پس که دستانِ خود را از اسارتِ خاک بازرهانید.

پس پُشته‌ها و خاک به اطاعتِ آدمی گردن نهادند * و کوه به اطاعتِ آدمی گردن نهاد * و دریاها و رود به اطاعتِ آدمی گردن نهادند * هم‌چنان که بیشه‌ها و باد * و آتش، آدمی را بنده شد * و از جانداران هرچه بود آدمی را بنده شدند، در آب و به خاک و بر آسمان؛ هرچه بودند و به هر کجای * و مُلکِ جهان او را شد * و پادشاهی‌ی آب و خاک، او را مسلم شد * و جهان به زیر نگین او شد به تمامی * و زمان در پنجه‌ی قدرت او قرار گرفت * و زرِّ آفتاب را سکّه به نامِ خویش کرد از آن پس که دستانِ خود را از بندگی‌ی خاک بازرهانید.

پس صورتِ خاک را بگردانید * و رود را و دریا را به مُهر خویش داغ برنهاد به غلامی * و به هر جای، با نهادِ خاک پنجه در پنجه کرد به ظفر * و زمین را یک‌سره بازآفرید به دستان * و خدای را، هم به دستان؛ به خاک و به چوب و به خرسنگ * و به حیرت در آفریده‌ی خویش نظر کرد، چرا که با زیبائی‌ی دست‌کارِ او زیبائی‌ی هیچ آفریده به کس نبود * و او را نماز بُرد، چرا که معجزه‌ی دستانِ او بود از آن پس که از اسارتِ خاکِشان وارهانید.

پس خدای را که آفریده‌ی دستانِ معجزگر او بود با اندیشه‌ی خویش وانهاد * و دستانِ خدای‌آفرین خود را که سلاحِ پادشاهی‌ی او بودند به درگاهِ او گسیل کرد به گدائی‌ی نیاز و برکت.

کفرانِ نعمت شد * و دستانِ توهین شده آدمی را لعنت کردند چرا که مُقامِ ایشان بر سینه نبود به بندگی.

و تباهی آغاز یافت.

۴ دی ۱۳۴۳

...And So Began the Ruin

Then he stood firm upon the earth * straightened his spine * raised his neck in pride and cried: Behold me! Man! Lord of the earth!

And all the living creatures feared his roar * and the pride concealed in that roar overcame them all * Man left the animals behind * surpassed them * and was lord over them after freeing his hands from the captivity of the earth.

Then the hills and the earth bowed in submission to man * the mountain bowed in submission * the seas and rivers submitted * as did the forests and the wind * Fire bent to his will * and every living creature in water, on land, or in the sky, no matter where and what, became his subject * The dominion of the world became his * sovereignty over land and water firmly his * Under his seal, the world was his * and time fell into his grasp * He minted the sun's gold into coins bearing his name after freeing his hands from the bondage of the earth.

Then he transformed the face of the earth * and branded rivers and seas with his seal of servitude * Everywhere, he wrestled with the earth's essence and triumphed * He recreated the land with his hands * and with those hands he created God from earth, wood, and rock * He marveled at his creation, for no beauty rivaled the beauty crafted by his hands * He worshiped it, the miracle of his hands, after freeing them from the captivity of the earth.

Then he reasoned to abandon God, the very creation of his miracle-making hands * and he sent forth those same hands, the weapons of his lordship, to God's altar, begging for blessings and bread.

He committed the Sin of Ingratitude, and squandered them * And the insulted hands cursed mankind, for their place was not on the chest in servitude.

And so began the ruin.

December 25, 1964

غزلی در نتوانستن

از دست‌های گرمِ تو
کودکانِ توأمانِ آغوشِ خویش
سخن‌ها می‌توانم گفت
غمِ نان اگر بگذارد.

□

نغمه در نغمه درافکنده
ای مسیح مادر، ای خورشید!
از مهربانیِی بی‌دریغ جانات
با چنگِ تمامی‌ناپذیرِ تو سرودها می‌توانم کرد
غمِ نان اگر بگذارد.

□

رنگ‌ها در رنگ‌ها دویده،
از رنگین‌کمانِ بهاریِ تو
که سراپرده در این باغِ خزان رسیده برافراشته است
نقش‌ها می‌توانم زد
غمِ نان اگر بگذارد.

□

چشمه‌ساری در دل و
آبشاری در کف،
آفتابی در نگاه و
فرشته‌ئی در پیراهن،
از انسانی که توئی
قصه‌ها می‌توانم کرد
غمِ نان اگر بگذارد.

۱۳ دیِ ۱۳۴۳

If Only

If only the burden of bread
would let me,
I'd speak volumes
of your warm hands—
two toddlers tangled in my arms.

☐

Songs fold into songs—
O mother of Christ, O sun!
I'd write songs
of your boundless heart
strumming its endless harp
if only the burden of bread
would let me.

☐

Colors blur into colors—
I'd paint patterns
of your springtime rainbow,
pitched like a canopy
over the fall-stricken garden
if only the burden of bread
would let me.

☐

You are a wellspring in the heart,
                             a waterfall in my hands
a sun in my eyes,
an angel in disguise.
I'd tell tales
of the human that you are
if only the burden of bread
would let me.

January 3, 1965

قُقنوس در باران
۱۳۴۵

Phoenix in the Rain

1966

رود

خویشتن را به بسترِ تقدیر سپردن
و با هر سنگ‌ریزه
رازی به نارضائی گفتن.

زمزمه‌یِ رود چه شیرین است!

□

از تیزه‌هایِ غرورِ خویش فرود آمدن
و از دل پاکی‌هایِ سرفرازِ انزوا به زیرافتادن
با فریادی از وحشتِ هر سقوط.

غرشِ آب‌شاران چه شکوه‌مند است!

□

و هم‌چنان در شیبِ شیار فروتر نشستن
و با هر خرسنگ
به جدالی برخاستن.

چه حماسه‌ئی‌ست رود، چه حماسه‌ئی‌ست!

۵ بهمنِ ۱۳۴۴

River

To surrender to the bedrock of destiny
spilling hesitant secrets
to every stone.

How sweet the river's murmur!

☐

To plummet from the spikes of pride
to crash from the purity of solitude,
a cry tearing through every fall.

How glorious the thunder of waterfalls!

☐

And to keep plunging down the ravine
only to rise and fight
every boulder in your path.

What an epic the river is—what an epic!

January 25, 1966

مرثیه‌هایِ خاک

۱۳۴۸

Elegies of the Earth

1969

مرثیه

در خاموشی‌یِ فروغ فرخزاد

به جُست‌وجویِ تو
بر درگاهِ کوه می‌گریم،
در آستانه‌یِ دریا و علف.

به جُست‌وجویِ تو
در معبرِ بادها می‌گریم،
در چاراَراهِ فصول،
در چارچوبِ شکسته‌یِ پنجره‌ئی
که آسمانِ ابرآلوده را
    قابی کهنه می‌گیرد.

. . . .

به انتظارِ تصویرِ تو
این دفترِ خالی
    تا چند
        تا چند
    ورق خواهد خورد؟

◻

جریانِ باد را پذیرفتن
و عشق را
که خواهرِ مرگ است. ـ
و جاودانه‌گی
    رازش را
با تو در میان نهاد.

پس به هیأتِ گنجی درآمدی:
بایسته و آزانگیز
    گنجی از آن دست
که تملکِ خاک را و دیاران را
    از این‌سان
دل‌پذیر کرده است!

Elegy

On the passing of Forough Farrokhzad

Searching for you
I weep at the foothills,
at the threshold of grass and sea.

Searching for you
I weep where the winds collide,
where the seasons cross,
within the cracked frame of a window,
its weathered wood holding
a sky stained with clouds.

. . . .

How long,
how long
will these empty pages turn,
waiting for your reflection?

☐

To embrace the way of the wind
and of love—sister to death.
Immortality
shared its secret with you.

So you became a treasure
worthy and sought,
the kind that makes belonging
to this earth and these lands feel so right.

☐

Your name is the dawn crossing the sky—
bless your name

□

نام‌ات سپیده‌دمی‌ست که بر پیشانی‌یِ آسمان می‌گذرد
— متبرک باد نامِ تو! —

و ما هم‌چنان
دوره می‌کنیم
شب را و روز را
هنوز را...

۲۹ بهمنِ ۱۳۴۵

And still
we go on
through the night and the day
and into the now

    February 18, 1967

هملت

بودن
یا نبودن...

بحث در این نیست
وسوسه این است.

□

شرابِ زهرآلوده به جام و
شمشیرِ به زهر آب‌دیده
در کفِ دشمن. —

همه چیزی
از پیش
روشن است و حساب‌شده
و پرده
در لحظه‌یِ معلوم
فرو خواهد افتاد.

پدرم مگر به باغِ **جتسمانی** خفته بود
که نقشِ من میراثِ اعتمادِ فریب‌کارِ اوست
و بسترِ فریبِ او
کام‌گاهِ عموی‌ام!
[من این همه را
به‌ناگهان دریافتم،
با نیم‌نگاهی
از سرِ اتفاق
به نظّاره‌گانِ تماشا]

اگر اعتماد
چون شیطانی دیگر
این **هابیل** دیگر را
به **جتسمانی** دیگر
به بی‌خبری لالا نگفته بود، —

Hamlet

To be
or not to be...

That is not the question—
It's the temptation

☐

Poisoned wine in the goblet,
venom-tempered sword
                in the enemy's hand—

everything pre-calculated
                and clear,
and the curtain
         will drop
                on cue.

Was it because my father had fallen asleep in the Garden of Gethsemane
that my fate is to inherit his betrayed trust,
his bed of betrayal—
                the seat of my uncle's pleasure?!
(I grasped it all
in an instant
with just a half-glance,
by sheer chance,
at the crowd)

If only trust,
    like another demon,
hadn't lulled to sleep
this other, unaware Abel
        in the other Gethsemane—

خدا را
خدا را!

□

چه فریبی اما،
چه فریبی!
که آن که از پسِ پرده‌ی نیم‌رنگِ ظلمت به تماشا نشسته
از تمامی‌ی فاجعه
آگاه است
و غم‌نامه‌ی مرا
پیشاپیش
حرف به حرف
بازمی‌شناسد.

□

در پسِ پرده‌ی نیم‌رنگِ تاریکی
چشم‌ها
نظاره‌ی دردِ مرا

سکه‌ها از سیم و زر پرداخته‌اند
تا از طرحِ آزادِ گریستن
در اختلالِ صدا و تنفسِ آن کس
که متظاهرانه
در حقیقت به تردید می‌نگرد
لذتی به کف آرند.

از اینان مدد از چه خواهم، که سرانجام
مرا و عموی مرا
به تساوی
در برابرِ خویش به کُرنش می‌خوانند،
هرچند رنجِ من ایشان را ندا دردداده باشد که دیگر
کلادیوس
نه نامِ عمّ
که مفهومی‌ست عام.

My god
My god!

☐

And what deceit,
                  what deceit!
that the one watching from behind the half-lit curtain of darkness
already knows everything—
the entire tragedy,
and every word
                  of my gospel of grief.

☐

Behind the half-lit curtain of darkness
                  those eyes
                          witnessing the spectacle of my anguish
paid in silver and gold
to take pleasure
in the display of open tears,
in the halting gasps of the one
pretending
to doubt the truth.

Why should I turn to those who, in the end,
demand that both my uncle and I
                  bow before them equally,
even though my suffering
was a clue they ignored,
that Claudius
                is no longer just an uncle's name,
but a universal notion.

و پرده...
در لحظه‌یِ محتوم...

□

با این همه
از آن زمان که حقیقت
چون روحِ سرگردانِ بی‌آرامی بر من آشکاره شد
و گندِ جهان
چون دودِ مشعلی در صحنه‌هایِ دروغین
منخرینِ مرا آزرد،
بحثی نه
که وسوسه‌ئی‌ست این:

بودن
    یا
نبودن.

۱۳۴۸

And the curtain...
in the fateful moment...

    ☐

Despite it all
            ever since the moment of truth
revealed itself like a restless spirit
and the stench of the world
stung my nostrils
            like smoke from a flame in a farce,
it has never been a question,
            but a temptation, this:

To be
or
not to be.

1969

شکُفتن در مه
۱۳۴۹

Blossoming in the Mist

1970

نامه

بدان زمان که شود تیره روزگار، پدر!
سراب و هستو روشن شود به پیشِ نظر.

مرا – به جانِ تو – از دیرباز می‌دیدم
که روزِ تجربه از یاد می‌بری یک‌سر
سلاح مردمی از دست می‌گذاری باز
به دلَ نمانَد هیچ‌ات ز رادمردی اثر

مرا به دامِ عدو مانده‌ای به کامِ عدو
بدان امید که رادی نهم ز دست مگر؟
نه گفته بودم صد ره که نان و نور، مرا
گر از طریق بپیچم شرنگِ باد و شرر؟

کنون من ایدر در حبس و بندِ خصم نی‌اَم
که بند بگسلد از پای من بخواهم اگر:
به سایه‌دستی بندم ز پای بگشاید
به سایه‌دستی بردارَدَم کلون از در.

من از بلندی‌یِ ایمانِ خویشتن ماندم
در این بلند که سیمرغ را بریزد پر.
چه درد اگر تو به خود می‌زنی به درد انگشت؟
چه سجن اگر تو به خود می‌کنی به سجن مقر؟
به پهن دریا دیدی که مردمِ چالاک
برآورند ز اعماقِ آبِ تیره دُرَر

به قصه نیز شنیدی که رفت و در ظلمات
کنارِ چشمه‌یِ جاوید جُست اسکندر
هم این ترانه شنفتی که حق و جاهِ کسان
نمی‌دهند کسان را به تخت و در بستر.

نه سعدِ سلمان‌ام من که ناله بردارم
که پستی آمد از این برکشیده با من بر.
چو گاهِ رفعت‌ام از رفعتی نصیب نبود
کنون چه مویم کافتاده‌ام به پست اندر؟

Letter

Father,

When things get hard, truth doesn't hide—
it stares you down. I've known this all along. But you?

You vanish every time. Once again, you've dropped the fight,
run off with your courage nowhere in sight, leaving me

tangled in the enemy's trap, in hopes I'll quit. But I've told you, again
and again, that it's not power I crave, but bread and light.

Here I stand, unchained, unafraid. One signature, that's all
it'd take to unbolt my prison door. I've stood so tall, so high

even the great Simorgh's wings—strong as they are—
would shed their feathers, and fall.

What's a little self-inflicted pain?
Or a self-built prison you call home?

You've seen the brave dive deep and surface
pearls from the darkest waters. You've heard that Alexander chased

immortality at the eternal spring. You know the ranks you treasure most
aren't born of beds or thrones.

But I'm no Salman the poet, crying over a fall from court
caused by well-placed, propped-up pawns.

مرا حکایتِ پیرار و پار پنداری
ز یاد رفته که با ما نه خشک بود نه تر؟
نه جخ شباهتِ‌مان با درختِ باروری
که یک بدان سال افتاده از ثمر دیگر،
که سالیانِ دراز است کاین حکایتِ فقر
حکایتی‌ست که تکرار می‌شود به کرر.

نه فقر، باش بگویم‌ات چیست تا دانی:
وقیح‌مایه درختی که می‌شکوفد بر
در آن وقاحتِ شورابه، کز خجالتِ آب
به تنگ‌بالی بر خاک تن زند آذر!

تو هم به پرده‌یِ مائی پدر. مگردان راه
مکن نوای غریبانه سر به زیر و زبر.
چه‌ت اوفتاده؟ که می‌ترسی ار گشائی چشم
تو را مِس آید رؤیای پُرتلألؤ زر؟
چه‌ت اوفتاده؟ که می‌ترسی ار به خود جُنبی
ز عرشِ شعله درافتی به فرشِ خاکستر؟
به وحشتی که بیفتی ز تختِ چوبیِ خویش
به خاک ریزدت احجارِ کاغذین‌افسر؟

تو را که کسوتِ زرتارِ زرپرستی نیست
کلاهِ خویش‌پرستی چه می‌نهی بر سر؟
تو را که پایه بر آب است و کارمایه خراب
چه پی فکندن در سیل‌بارِ این بندر؟
تو کز معامله جز باد دستگیرت نیست
حدیثِ بادفروشان چه می‌کنی باور؟

حکایتی عجب است این! ندیده‌ای که چه‌سان
به تیغِ کینه فکندندِمان به کوی و گذر؟
چراغِ علم ندیدی به هر کجا کُشتند
زدندَ آتش هر جا به نامه و دفتر؟

Fate didn't grant me the heights I sought—
so why should I grieve the fall? We've all been

crushed, year after year, but I don't forget. We're like that tree—
fruit-laden one season, barren the next.

It's not poverty, Father—it's shame: it's a tale of a tree that self-combusts
too proud to drink from the shameless swamp.

You're one of us, Father, dear. So why sing out of tune?
Why can't you face the truth?

Why do you so fear to leave the burning heights, to lose
your wooden throne and the jewels of its paper crown?

You've gained nothing but wind, yet you trust
the windbags who sold it to you. They've cut

us down with their hate, snuffed out knowledge, torched our books.
The blood of my comrades soaks the earth—

don't turn your cold gaze on this red dawn.
Check the chronicles of the East—each page tells of a new win.

In Gilan, my friends bled, yet stood strong in their cells. You'd have me
grovel and beg, write a plea that makes our enemy feel smug?

Save my skin but sell my soul, trade truth for lies?
Should I turn away from the sunrise and sink

زمین ز خونِ رفیقانِ من خضاب گرفت
چنین به سردی در سرخی‌ی شفق منگر!
یکی به دفترِ مشرقِ بیین پدر، که نبشت
به هر صحیفه سرودی ز فتحِ تازه بشر!

□

بدان زمان که به گیلان به خاک و خون غلتند
به پای‌مردی، یارانِ من به زندان در،
مرا تو درسِ فرومایه بودن آموزی
که توبه‌نامه نویسم به کامِ دشمن بر؟
نجاتِ تن را زنجیرِ روحِ خویش کنم
ز راستی بنشانم فریب را برتر؟
ز صبحِ تابان برتابم – ای دریغا – روی
به شامِ تیره‌ی رو در سفر سپارم سر؟
قبای دیبه به مسکوکِ قلب بفروشم
شرف سرانه دهم وان‌گهی خرم جُلِ خر؟

□

مرا به پندِ فرومایه جانِ خود مگزای
که تفته نایدم آهن بدین حقیر آذر:
تو راهِ راحتِ جان گیر و من مقامِ مصاف
تو جای امن و امان گیر و من طریقِ خطر!

۱۳۳۳
زندانِ قصر

into the oncoming dark? Sell my honor for fool's gold?
Don't weigh me down with weak advice.

You amble along your peaceful road. Me,
I'll walk danger's path.

1954
Qasr prison

عقوبت

برای ایرج گُردی

میوه بر شاخه شدم
سنگ‌پاره در کفِ کودک.
طلسمِ معجزتی
مگر پناه دهد از گزندِ خویشتن‌ام
چنین که
دستِ تطاول به خود گشاده
من‌ام!

▫

بالا بلند!
بر جلوخانِ منظرم
چون گردشِ اطلسیِ ابر
قدم بردار.

از هجومِ پرنده‌ی بی‌پناهی
چون به خانه بازآیم
پیش از آن که در بگشایم
بر تختگاهِ ایوان
جلوه‌ئی کن
با رُخساری که باران و زمزمه است.
چنان کن که مجالی اَندَکَک را درخور است،
که تبردارِ واقعه را
دیگر
دستِ خسته
به فرمان
نیست.

▫

که گفته است
من آخرین بازمانده‌ی فرزانه‌گانِ زمین‌ام؟ –

The Price

For Iraj Gordi

I became fruit on the branch,
                      a stone in a child's hand.
May a miraculous spell
protect me from harm at my own hands
in the war
        I've waged against
                 myself!

☐

Tall beauty,
move before my eyes
like clouds gliding
          smooth as silk.

When I return home
          from the onslaught of a nestless bird,
before I open the door,
let me find you
          on the throne of the veranda,
                  your face a whisper, a rain.
Take this ever so slight chance,
because the ax-wielder's tired hand
               can no longer
steer the course of fate.

☐

Who says
I'm the last wise soul on earth?

من آن غولِ زیبای‌ام که در استوایِ شب ایستاده است
غریقِ زلالی‌یِ همه آب‌هایِ جهان،
و چشم‌اندازِ شیطنت‌اش
خاست‌گاهِ ستاره‌ئی‌ست.

در انتهایِ زمین‌ام کومه‌ئی هست، ــ
آن‌جا که
پادرجائی‌یِ خاک
هم‌چون رقصِ سراب
بر فریبِ عطش
تکیه می‌کند.

در مفصلِ انسان و خدا
آری
در مفصلِ خاک و پوک‌ام کومه‌ئی ناستوار هست،
و بادی که بر لُجِّه‌یِ تاریک می‌گذرد
بر ایوانِ بی‌رونقِ سردم
جاروب می‌کشد.

برده‌گانِ عالی‌جاه را دیده‌ام من
در کاخ‌هایِ بلند
که قلاده‌هایِ زرین به گردن داشته‌اند
و آزاده مَردُم را
در جامه‌هایِ مرقع
که سرودگویان
پیاده به مقتل می‌رفته‌اند.

□

خانه‌یِ من در انتهایِ جهان است
در مفصلِ خاک و
پوک.

با ما گفته بودند:

I'm the beautiful giant standing on night's equator,
                              drowned in the clarity of the world's waters,
my mischief reaching
the birthplace of stars.

At the edge of my land, stands a shed
where the earth's permanence—
                       like a dancing mirage—
relies on the illusion
         of thirst.

At the crossroads of man and god—
yes, where my earth meets dust—
stands an unsteady shed,
and the wind from the dark abyss
                       sweeps across my cold, empty porch.

I've seen noble slaves
in grand palaces,
golden chains around their necks,
and free souls in rags,
singing anthems
as they marched to their deaths.

     ☐

My home sits at the world's edge
where earth meets dust.

They told us:
         We'll teach you
         the sacred word,
         but for it,

«آن کلامِ مقدس را
با شما خواهیم آموخت،
لیکن به خاطرِ آن
عقوبتی جان‌فرسای را
تحمل می‌بایدِتان کرد.»

عقوبتِ جان‌کاه را چندان تاب آوردیم
آری
که کلامِ مقدسِ‌مان
باری
از خاطر
گریخت!

۱۳۴۹

you must pay
a soul-crushing price.

And we paid that price for so long
that, yes,
the sacred word
did indeed slip away
from our minds!

1971

ابراهیم در آتش
۱۳۵۲

Abraham in Flames

1973

شبانه (در نیست)

در نیست
راه نیست
شب نیست
ماه نیست
نه روز و
نه آفتاب،
ما
بیرونِ زمان
ایستاده‌ایم
با دشنه‌ی تلخی
در گُرده‌هایِ‌مان.

هیچ‌کس
با هیچ‌کس
سخن نمی‌گوید
که خاموشی
به هزار زبان
در سخن است.
در مردگانِ خویش
نظر می‌بندیم
با طرحِ خنده‌ئی،
و نوبتِ خود را انتظار می‌کشیم
بی‌هیچ
خنده‌ئی!

۱۵ فروردینِ ۱۳۵۱

Nocturnal (There's No Door)

There's no door
                no route
no night
                no moon
no day
                no sun
We stand
                beyond time,
a bitter dagger
in our backs.

No one
                speaks
                          to anyone
because silence
                speaks
                          in a thousand tongues.
We stare
                at our dead
                          wearing a smile,
waiting
our turn—
without
a smile!

        April 4, 1972

شبانه (اگر که بیهده زیباست شب)

اگر که بیهده زیباست شب
برایِ چه زیباست
شب
برایِ که زیباست؟ –

شب و
رودِ بی‌انحنایِ ستاره‌گان
که سرد می‌گذرد.

و سوگوارانِ درازگیسو
بر دو جانبِ رود
یادآوردِ کدام خاطره را
با قصیده‌یِ نفس‌گیرِ غوکان
تعزیتی می‌کنند
به هنگامی که هر سپیده
به صدایِ هم‌آوازِ دوازده گلوله
سوراخ
می‌شود؟

□

اگر که بیهده زیباست شب
برایِ که زیباست شب
برایِ چه زیباست؟

۲۶ اسفندِ ۱۳۵۰

Nocturnal (If Night is Beautiful in Vain)

If night is beautiful in vain
then why is it beautiful at all
                      night—
for whom is it beautiful?

Night
        and the unbending river of stars
passing cold and still.

And which memory
                do the long-haired mourners
on both banks of the river mourn
                      with the breathtaking elegy of frogs,
as each dawn is pierced
with a chorus of twelve gunshots?

☐

If night is beautiful in vain
then for whom is it beautiful, night—
why is it beautiful at all?

    March 17, 1972

شبانه (بی‌سببی)

مرا
تو
بی‌سببی
نیستی.

به‌راستی
صلتِ کدام قصیده‌ای
ای غزل؟
ستاره‌بارانِ جوابِ کدام سلامی
به آفتاب
از دریچه‌ی تاریک؟

کلام از نگاهِ تو شکل می‌بندد.
خوشا نظربازی‌ا که تو آغاز می‌کنی!

□

پسِ پُشتِ مردمکانات
فریادِ کدام زندانی‌ست
که آزادی را
به لبانِ برآماسیده
گُلِ سرخی پرتاب می‌کند؟ –
ورنه
این ستاره‌بازی
حاشا
چیزی بده‌کارِ آفتاب نیست.

□

نگاه از صدای تو ایمن می‌شود.
چه مؤمنانه نامِ مرا آواز می‌کنی!

□

و دل‌ات
کبوترِ آشتی‌ست،

Nocturnal (You Didn't Just Happen to Me)

You
       didn't just
happen
       to me.

Really,
       you, my ghazal—
what qasideh could ever measure up to you?
What dazzling salute to the sun
are you
       from the pitch dark?

Your gaze brings words to life.
Lucky the games of glances that you spark!

☐

Behind your pupils,
which prisoner,
       lips swollen,
throws a red rose
       to freedom with their cry?
Because
       this play of light
owes nothing
       to the sun.

☐

Your voice shelters the gaze.
How faithfully you call my name!

☐

And your heart,
is a dove of peace

در خون تپیده
به بامِ تلخ.

با این همه
چه بالا
چه بلند
پرواز می‌کنی!

فروردینِ ۱۳۵۱

beating in blood
against the bitter rooftop.

Yet how high
how far
you fly!

    April 1972

سرودِ ابراهیم در آتش

اعدامِ مهدی رضائی در میدانِ تیرِ چیتگر

در آوارِ خونینِ گرگ و میش
دیگرگونه مردیَ آنک،
که خاک را سبز می‌خواست
و عشق را شایسته‌ی زیباترینِ زنان
که این‌اش
به نظر
هدیّتی نه چندان کم‌بها بود
که خاک و سنگ را بشاید.

چه مردی! چه مردی!
که می‌گفت
قلب را شایسته‌تر آن
که به هفت شمشیرِ عشق
در خون نشیند

و گلو را بایسته‌تر آن
که زیباترینِ نام‌ها را
بگوید.
و شیرآهن‌کوه مردی از این‌گونه عاشق
میدانِ خونین سرنوشت
به **پاشنه‌ی آشیل**
درنوشت. —

روئینه‌تنی
که رازِ مرگ‌اش
اندوهِ عشق و
غمِ تنهائی بود.

□

«— آه، اسفندیارِ مغموم!
تو را آن به که چشم
فروپوشیده باشی!»

The Anthem of Abraham in Flames

The execution of Mehdi Rezaei at Chitgar shooting grounds

In the bloody aftermath of twilight
stood another kind of man—
a man who wanted the earth green
and love worthy of the fairest women.
To him,
this was no trivial gift
fit for just dirt and stone.

What a man! What a man, who said:
the heart is meant for more
                        than being pierced and bloodied
by the seven swords of love,
and the throat for greater deeds
than to only utter the most beautiful names.

A lionhearted titan
towering man of iron
who loved with ferocity,
who walked the blood-soaked field of destiny
                        on an Achilles' heel—
an invincible being
                whose secret of death
was the sorrow of love
and the pain of solitude.

    ☐

"Oh, sad Esfandiar!
It's better
that you avert your eyes!"

«- آیا نه
یکی **نه**
بسنده بود
که سرنوشتِ مرا بسازد؟

من
تنها فریاد زدم
نه!
من از
فرورفتن
تن زدم.

صدائی بودم من
ـ شکلی میانِ اشکال ـ ،
و معنائی یافتم.

من **بودم**
و **شدم**،
نه زان‌گونه که غنچه‌ئی
گُلی
یا ریشه‌ئی
که جوانه‌ئی
یا یکی دانه
که جنگلی ـ
راست بدان‌گونه
که عامی‌مردی
شهیدی؛
تا آسمان بر او نماز بَرَد.

من بی‌نوا بنده‌گکی سربه‌راه
نبودم

☐

"Was a *no*,
        a single *no*
                enough to forge my destiny?

I simply cried out,
        no!
I refused
        to sink into submission.

I was a voice,
a form among forms,
and I gained meaning.

I was,
and I became—
not as a bud becomes a rose,
or a root a sprout,
or a single seed a forest,
but as a common man becomes a martyr,
making the heavens bow down to him in prayer.

I was no meek, obedient slave,
and the path to my celestial heaven
wasn't one of submission and servility.
I needed a different kind of god—
a god worthy of a creation
                that doesn't bow
                          for a fated morsel.

And so I created
a different kind of god."

☐

و راهِ بهشتِ مینویِ من
بُزرو طوع و خاک‌ساری
نبود:
مرا دیگرگونه خدائی می‌بایست
شایسته‌یِ آفرینه‌ئی
که نواله‌یِ ناگزیر را
گردن
کج نمی‌کند.

و خدائی
دیگرگونه
آفریدم)».

□

دریغا شیرآهن‌کوه مردا
که تو بودی،
و کوه‌وار
پیش از آن که به خاک افتی
نستوه و استوار
مُرده بودی.
اما نه خدا و نه شیطان —
سرنوشتِ تو را
بُتی رقم زد
که دیگران
می‌پرستیدند.
بُتی که
دیگران‌اش
می‌پرستیدند.

۱۳۵۲

Oh, lionhearted titan,
                you were,
before falling to earth—
                mountain-like, steadfast, and strong—
                              already dead.
Yet, neither God nor Satan
sealed your fate,
            but an idol
that others worshiped—
            an idol
                      worshiped by others.

1973

ترانه‌ی تاریک

بر زمینه‌ی سُربی‌یِ صبح
سوار
خاموش ایستاده است
و یالِ بلندِ اسب‌اش در باد
پریشان می‌شود.

□

خدایا خدایا
سواران نباید ایستاده باشند
هنگامی که
حادثه اخطار می‌شود.

□

کنارِ پرچینِ سوخته
دختر
خاموش ایستاده است
و دامنِ نازک‌اش در باد
تکان می‌خورد.

خدایا خدایا
دختران نباید خاموش بمانند
هنگامی که مردان
نومید و خسته
پیر می‌شوند.

۱۳۵۲

Dark Song

Against the leaden dawn
the rider
   stands still,
his horse's long mane wild
      in the wind.

☐

O Lord, O Lord,
riders must not stand still
when the moment nears.

☐

By the burnt hedge
the girl
   stands still,
her thin skirt trembling
      in the wind.

O Lord, O Lord
girls must not stand still
when hopeless,
tired men
   grow old.

1973

بر سرمایِ درون

همه
لرزشِ دست و دل‌ام
از آن بود
که عشق
پناهی گردد،
پروازی نه
گریزگاهی گردد.

آی عشق آی عشق
چهره‌یِ آبی‌ات پیدا نیست.

□

و خنکایِ مرهمی
بر شعله‌یِ زخمی
نه شورِ شعله
بر سرمایِ درون.

آی عشق آی عشق
چهره‌یِ سُرخ‌ات پیدا نیست.

□

غبارِ تیره‌یِ تسکینی
بر حضورِ وَهن
و دنجِ رهائی
بر گریزِ حضور،
سیاهی
بر آرامشِ آبی
و سبزه‌یِ برگچه
بر ارغوان

آی عشق آی عشق
رنگِ آشنای‌ات
پیدا نیست.

۱۳۵۲

On the Winter Within

All
    the trembling in me
               was for love
to be a refuge—
        not a flight,
but a sanctuary.

Oh love, oh love
Your blue face is nowhere to be found.

☐

A cooling balm
        on the fire of a wound—
not a raging flame
on the winter within.

Oh love, oh love
Your red face is nowhere to be found.

☐

A dark dust of solace
            on the weight of the mundane,
a quiet release
        from the flight of existence.
Blackness
      over quiet blue,
tender greens
      on a violet bloom.

Oh love, oh love
Your familiar color is nowhere to be found.

    1973

از این گونه مُردن...

می‌خواهم خوابِ اقاقیاها را بمیرم.

خیال‌گونه
در نسیمی کوتاه
که به تردید می‌گذرد
خوابِ اقاقیاها را
بمیرم.

▫

می‌خواهم نفسِ سنگینِ اطلسی‌ها را پرواز گیرم.

در باغچه‌های تابستان،
خیس و گرم
به نخستین ساعاتِ عصر
نفس اطلسی‌ها را
پرواز گیرم.

▫

حتا اگر
زنبقِ کبودِ کارد
بر سینه‌ام
گُل دهد –
می‌خواهم خوابِ اقاقیاها را بمیرم در آخرین فرصتِ گُل،
و عبورِ سنگینِ اطلسی‌ها باشم
بر تالارِ ارسی
به ساعتِ هفتِ عصر.

۱۸ آبانِ ۱۳۵۱

To Die This Way…

I want to die like the dream of acacias—

entranced
as a fleeting breeze
                    passing softly—
to die
like the dream of acacias.

☐

I want to ride the heavy breath of petunias—

across damp and warm
summer lawns
                in the first bloom of afternoon—
to ride
the breath of petunias.

☐

Even if
      the blue iris of the blade
blooms
on my chest—
still, I want to die like the dream of acacias in the flower's final chance,
to drift, heavy as petunias
across a stained-glass hall
at seven as evening falls.

November 8, 1972

اشارتی

به ایران درودی

پیش از تو
صورت‌گران
بسیار
از آمیزه‌ی برگ‌ها
آهوان برآوردند؛
یا در خطوطِ کوهپایه‌ئی
رمه‌ئی
که شبان‌اش در کج و کوجِ ابر و ستیغِ کوه
نهان است؛

یا به سیری و سادگی
در جنگلِ پُرنگارِ مه‌آلود
گوزنی را گرسنه
که ماغ می‌کشد.

تو خطوطِ شباهت را تصویر کن:
آه و آهن و آهکِ زنده
دود و دروغ و درد را. –
که خاموشی
تقوایِ ما نیست.

□

سکوتِ آب
می‌تواند خشکی باشد و فریادِ عطش؛
سکوتِ گندم
می‌تواند گرسنگی باشد و غریوِ پیروزمندِ قحط؛
هم‌چنان که سکوتِ آفتاب
ظلمات است –
اما سکوتِ آدمی فقدانِ جهان و خداست:
غریو را
تصویر کن!

Edict

To Iran Darroudi

Before you,
many painters
brought gazelles to life
        from a mix of leaves,
or herds
grazing in the folds of hills,
their shepherd tucked
        in the curve of clouds and the mountain peaks.
Or in simple, sated ease
a hungry deer bleating
in the misty vivid forest.

Why don't you draw the lines of likeness—
sighs, steel, and quicklime,
smoke, suffering, and deceit—
because silence
        isn't our virtue.

☐

The absence of water
could mean drought, the cry of thirst
The absence of wheat
could mean hunger, famine's win,
just as the absence of the sun
        is darkness.
But the absence of humanity—
that's when the world,
when God, is gone.
Why don't you draw that cry!

عصرِ مرا
در منحنیِ تازیانه به نیشِ‌خطِ رنج؛
هم‌سایه‌ی مرا
بیگانه با امید و خدا؛
و حرمتِ ما را
که به دینار و درم برکشیده‌اند و فروخته.

□

تمامیِ الفاظِ جهان را در اختیار داشتیم و
آن نگفتیم
که به کار آید
چرا که تنها یک سخن
یک سخن در میانه نبود:
— آزادی!

ما نگفتیم
تو تصویرش کن!

۱۴ اسفندِ ۱۳۵۱

Or my era—
captured in the arc of a whip,
scarred by the sting of pain
Or my neighbor—
cut off from hope and God
Or our dignity—
stripped and sold for scraps.

☐

Every word in the world was within our reach,
yet we failed to speak
                the one that mattered.
One word,
        just one was missing—
Freedom!

We never said it.
Now it's yours to capture!

      March 5, 1973

دشنه در دیس

۱۳۵۶

Dagger in the Tray

1977

هنوزِ در فکرِ آن کلاغ‌ام...

برای اسماعیل خویی

هنوز
در فکرِ آن کلاغ‌ام در دره‌هایِ **یوش**:

با قیچی‌یِ سیاه‌اش
بر زردی‌یِ برشته‌یِ گندم‌زار
با خِش‌خِشی مضاعَف
از آسمانِ کاغذی‌یِ مات

قوسی بُرید کج،

و رو به کوهِ نزدیک
با غارِ غارِ خشکِ گلوی‌اش

چیزی گفت

که کوه‌ها
بی‌حوصله
در زلِّ آفتاب
تا دیرگاهی آن را
با حیرت
در کَلّه‌هایِ سنگی‌ی‌شان
تکرار می‌کردند.

□

گاهی سوآل می‌کنم از خود که
یک کلاغ
با آن حضورِ قاطعِ بی‌تخفیف
وقتی
صلاتِ ظهر
با رنگِ سوگوارِ مُصرّش
بر زردی‌یِ برشته‌یِ گندم‌زاری بال می‌کشد
تا از فرازِ چند سپیدار بگذرد،
با آن خروش و خشم
چه دارد بگوید
با کوه‌هایِ پیر
کاین عابدانِ خسته‌یِ خواب‌آلود
در نیم‌روزِ تابستانی
تا دیرگاهی آن را با هم
تکرار کنند؟

شهریورِ ۱۳۵۴

Still I Think of That Raven...

For Esmaeil Khoei

Still
I think of that raven over the valleys of Yush:

black shears
cutting a crooked arc
across the matte paper sky,
both wings rustling,
above a sun-scorched field of wheat,
and facing the mountain
                        letting out a croak
that the mountains, with awe,
lazily echoed, for a long while
in their stone skulls
                under the relentless sun.

☐

Sometimes I ask myself
                what a raven,
so sharp and unwavering in its presence,
its mourning cloak persistent,
                has to say
as it rises at midday prayer
with thunder and fury
above a sun-scorched field of wheat,
gliding over a few poplars,
to the old mountains,
those tired and drowsy worshipers,
that echo its cry in unison
long into the summer afternoon?

September 1975

خطابه‌ی تدفین

غافلان
هم‌سازند،
تنها توفان
کودکانِ ناهم‌گون می‌زاید.

هم‌ساز
سایه‌سانان‌اند،
محتاط
در مرزهایِ آفتاب.
در هیأتِ زندگان
مردگان‌اند.

وینان
دل به دریا افگنان‌اند،
به پایِ دارنده‌یِ آتش‌ها
زندگانی
دوشادوشِ مرگ
پیشاپیشِ مرگ
همواره زنده از آن سپس که با مرگ
و همواره بدان نام
که زیسته بودند،
که تباهی
از درگاهِ بلندِ خاطره‌شان
شرمسار و سرافکنده می‌گذرد.

کاشفانِ چشمه
کاشفانِ فروتنِ شوکران
جویندگانِ شادی
در مجْریِ آتش‌فشان‌ها

Funeral Address

The unknowing
are alike
Only the tempest
breeds peerless children.

Those alike
are shadow-like,
cautious
on the fringes of sunlight,
dead
in the guise of the living.

And these,
they are the throwers of caution to the wind,
guardians of fires,
the living
shoulder to shoulder with death,
marching ahead of death,
forever alive after death,
and forever by the name
with which they lived,
for ruin
passes under their towering vision
downcast and shamefaced.

Discoverers of the fountainhead,
humble discoverers of hemlock,
seekers of joy
in the volcanoes' path,

شعبده‌بازانِ لبخند
در شب‌کلاهِ درد
با جاپائی ژرف‌تر از شادی
در گذرگاهِ پرندگان.

□

در برابرِ تُندر می‌ایستند
خانه را روشن می‌کنند.
و می‌میرند.

۲۵ اردیبهشتِ ۱۳۵۴

magicians of smiles
in nightcaps of pain,
with footprints deeper than joy
in the flyways of birds.

    □

They brace thunder,
enlighten the house
and die.

May 15, 1975

شکاف

در اعدامِ خسرو گلسرخی

زاده شدن
بر نیزه‌ی تاریک
هم‌چون میلادِ گشاده‌ی زخمی.

سِفْرِ یگانه‌ی فرصت را
سراسر
در سلسله پیمودن.
بر شعله‌ی خویش
سوختن
تا جرقّه‌ی واپسین،
بر شعله‌ی حُرمتی
که در خاکِ راه‌اش
یافته‌اند
بردگان
این‌چنین.

این‌چنین سُرخ و لوند
بر خاربوته‌ی خون
شکفتن
وین‌چنین گردن‌فراز
بر تازیانه‌زارِ تحقیر
گذشتن
و راه را تا غایتِ نفرت
بریدن. ــ

آه، از که سخن می‌گویم؟
ما بی‌چرازندگان‌ایم
آنان به چرامرگِ خود آگاهان‌اند.

۱۳۵۴

The Chasm

On the execution of Khosrow Golesorkhi

To be born
upon the dark spear
like the gaping birth of a wound.

To live
the one and only
book of fate
entirely in chains.

To burn
like this
on one's own flame
down to the last spark,
on the flame of honor
that slaves found
in the dust
of the way-worn path.

To blossom
so red and tempting
on the thornbush of blood
and to cross
the thrashing-field of scorn
like this
head held up high
and to carve the path to the ends of hatred—

Ah, of whom am I speaking?
We live unaware of why
They die well aware of why.

1975

ترانه‌یِ بزرگ‌ترین آرزو

آه اگر آزادی سرودی می‌خواند
کوچک
هم‌چون گلوگاهِ پرنده‌ئی،
هیچ‌کجا دیواری فروریخته بر جای نمی‌ماند.

سالیانِ بسیار نمی‌بایست
دریافتن را
که هر ویرانه نشانی از غیابِ انسانی‌ست
که حضورِ انسان
آبادانی‌ست.

□

هم‌چون زخمی
همه عُمر
خونابه چکنده
هم‌چون زخمی
همه عُمر
به دردی خشک تپنده،
به نعره‌ئی
چشم بر جهان گشوده
به نفرتی
از خود شونده، –

غیابِ بزرگ چنین بود
سرگذشتِ ویرانه چنین بود.

□

آه اگر آزادی سرودی می‌خواند
کوچک
کوچک‌تر حتا
از گلوگاهِ یکی پرنده!

دیِ ۱۳۵۵
رم

Song of the Greatest Wish

Ah, if freedom could sing a song
so small,
        like a bird's throat,
no wall left in ruins would ever stand.

It wouldn't take years
              to see that
every ruin speaks of human absence
while every presence
        is renewal.

☐

Like a wound
        that bleeds
             all its life,
a wound
        that beats a dry pain
              all its life,
that opens its eyes to the world
            with a cry
and turns away from itself
        in hatred—

such was the great absence,
such was the story of ruin.

☐

Ah, if freedom could sing a song
so small,
smaller even
than a bird's tiny throat!

    January 1977
    Rome

ترانه‌هایِ کوچکِ غُربت
۱۳۵۹

Little Songs of Exile

1980

بچه‌های اعماق

گفتار برای یک ترانه، در شهادتِ احمد زیبرم
به علیرضا اسپهبد

در شهر بی‌خیابان می‌بالند
در شبکه‌ی مورگی‌ی پس‌کوچه و بُن‌بست،
آغشته‌ی دودِ کوره و قاچاق و زردزخم
قابِ رنگین در جیب و تیرکمان در دست،

بچه‌های اعماق
بچه‌های اعماق

باتلاقِ تقدیرِ بی‌ترحم در پیش و
دشنامِ پدرانِ خسته در پُشت،
نفرینِ مادرانِ بی‌حوصله در گوش و
هیچ از امید و فردا در مشت،

بچه‌های اعماق
بچه‌های اعماق

□

بر جنگلِ بی‌بهار می‌شکفند
بر درختانِ بی‌ریشه میوه می‌آرند،

بچه‌های اعماق
بچه‌های اعماق

با حنجره‌ی خونین می‌خوانند و از پا درآمدنا
درفشی بلند به کف دارند

کاوه‌های اعماق
کاوه‌های اعماق

۱۳۵۴

Children of the Depths

> Song lyrics on the martyrdom of Ahmad Zibaram
> To Alireza Espahbod

They grow up in a city without streets
in the capillaries of back alleys and dead-ends,
coated in kiln ash, contraband, and scabs,
painted knucklebone dice in their pockets and slingshots in hand

> *Children of the depths*
> *Children of the depths*

A merciless swamp of a fate ahead,
the vitriol of worn-out fathers behind,
the curses of fed-up mothers in their ears
and nothing of hope or tomorrow in their fists

> *Children of the depths*
> *Children of the depths*

☐

They blossom in forests without springs
and ripen on rootless trees

> *Children of the depths*
> *Children of the depths*

They sing with bleeding throats and in defeat
hold high a banner in hand

> *Kavehs of the depths*
> *Kavehs of the depths*

1975

ترانه‌ی کوچک

- تو کجائی؟
در گستره‌ی بی‌مرزِ این جهان
تو کجائی؟

- من در دوردست‌ترین جایِ جهان ایستاده‌ام:
کنارِ تو.

□

- تو کجائی؟
در گستره‌ی ناپاکِ این جهان
تو کجائی؟

- من در پاک‌ترین مقامِ جهان ایستاده‌ام:
بر سبزه‌شورِ این رودِ بزرگ که می‌سُراید
برایِ تو.

دی ۱۳۵۷
لندن

Little Song

— Where are you?
In the infinite vastness of this world,

                              where are you?

— I stand at the edge of the world:
right by your side.

☐
— Where are you?
In the tainted vastness of this world,

                              where are you?

— I stand where the earth is purest:
on the lush, green banks of this great river that sings
for you.

January 1979
London

هجرانی (سینِ هفتم)

سینِ هفتم
سیبِ سُرخی‌ست،
حسرتا
که مرا
نصیب
از این سُفره‌یِ سُنّت
سروری نیست.

شرابی مردافکن در جامِ هواست،
شگفتا
که مرا
بدین مستی
شوری نیست.

سبویِ سبزه‌پوش
در قابِ پنجره –
آه
چنان دورم
که گوئی جز نقشِ بی‌جانی نیست.
و کلامی مهربان
در نخستین دیدارِ بامدادی –
فغان
که در پسِ پاسخ و لب‌خند
دلِ خندانی نیست.

بهاری دیگر آمده است
آری
اما برایِ آن زمستان‌ها که گذشت
نامی نیست
نامی نیست.

اسفندِ ۱۳۵۷
لندن

Distance (The Seventh "S")

The seventh "S"
              is a red apple.
Alas,
      if only I shared
             in the joy
                    of this altar of tradition.

Wine potent enough to fell a man
fills the cup of the air—
            how strange
                  that I feel no thrill
                        in this drunkenness.

The green-glazed pitcher
                in the window frame—
ah,
I'm so far away now
              that it feels like a lifeless image.
A kind word
           at the break of dawn—
alas,
      behind the nod and smile
                there's no joy in the heart.

Another spring has come,
            yes,
but for those winters that have passed,
there is no name,
no name.

      March 1979
      London

در این بُن‌بست

دهانت را می‌بویند
مبادا که گفته باشی دوستت‌ات می‌دارم
دلت را می‌بویند

روزگارِ غریبی‌ست، نازنین

و عشق را
کنارِ تیرکِ راهبند
تازیانه می‌زنند.

عشق را در پستوی خانه نهان باید کرد

در این بُن‌بستِ کج و پیچِ سرما
آتش را
به سوخت‌بارِ سرود و شعر
فروزان می‌دارند.
به اندیشیدن خطر مکن.

روزگارِ غریبی‌ست، نازنین

آن که بر در می‌کوبد شباهنگام
به کُشتنِ چراغ آمده است.

نور را در پستوی خانه نهان باید کرد

آنک قصّابان‌اند
بر گذرگاه‌ها مستقر،
با کُنده و ساتوری خون‌آلود

روزگارِ غریبی‌ست، نازنین

و تبسم را بر لب‌ها جراحی می‌کنند
و ترانه را بر دهان.

شوق را در پستوی خانه نهان باید کرد

کبابِ قناری
بر آتشِ سوسن و یاس

روزگارِ غریبی‌ست، نازنین

In This Dead-End Street

They sniff your breath
to see if you've dared say I love you
They sniff your heart

These are strange times, my dear

They whip love
at the barricade post

We must hide love in the closet

In this icy, winding dead-end street
they feed their fire
     by burning
          poems and songs
Don't even risk thinking

These are strange times, my dear

The one who knocks in the dead
of night has come to kill the light

We must hide the light in the closet

Butchers stand
at crossroads
with bloodied cleavers and chopping blocks

These are strange times, my dear

They surgically slice smiles from lips
and songs from mouths

We must hide joy in the closet

Canaries roast
over a fire of jasmine and lilies

These are strange times, my dear

ابلیسِ پیروزمست
سورِ عزای ما را بر سفره نشسته است.

خدا را در پستوی خانه نهان باید کرد

۳۱ تیرِ ۱۳۵۸

Drunk on victory, Satan sits
at the feast of our mourning

                        We must hide God in the closet

July 22, 1979

عاشقانه (آن که می‌گوید دوست‌ات می‌دارم)

آن که می‌گوید دوست‌ات می‌دارم
خنیاگرِ غم‌گینی‌ست
که آوازش را از دست داده است.

ای کاش عشق را
زبانِ سخن بود

هزار کاکُلی‌یِ شاد
در چشمانِ توست
هزار قناری‌یِ خاموش
در گلویِ من.

عشق را
ای کاش زبانِ سخن بود

□

آن که می‌گوید دوست‌ات می‌دارم
دلِ اندُه‌گین شبی‌ست
که مهتاب‌اش را می‌جوید.

ای کاش عشق را
زبانِ سخن بود

هزار آفتابِ خندان در خرامِ توست
هزار ستاره‌یِ گریان
در تمنایِ من.

عشق را
ای کاش زبانِ سخن بود

۳۱ تیرِ ۱۳۵۸

Tenderly (The One Who Says I Love You)

The one who says I love you
is a sad street singer
who's lost his song.

> *If only love*
> *could speak*

There are a thousand joyous songbirds
               in your eyes,
a thousand silent canaries
in my throat.

> *If only*
> *love could speak*

☐

The one who says I love you
is the grief-stricken heart
of a night seeking its moonlight.

> *If only love*
> *could speak*

A thousand smiling suns in your stride,
a thousand weeping stars
in my pleas.

> *If only*
> *love could speak*

July 22, 1979

شبانه (نه تو را برنتراشیده‌ام)

نه
تو را بر نتراشیده‌ام از حسرت‌هایِ خویش:
پارینه‌تر از سنگ
تُردتر از ساقه‌یِ تازه‌رویِ یکی علف.

تو را برنکشیده‌ام از خشمِ خویش:
ناتوانی‌یِ خِرَد
از برآمدن،
گُر کشیدن
در مجمرِ بی‌تابی.

تو را بر نَسَخته‌ام به وزنه‌یِ اندوهِ خویش:
پَرِّ کاهی
در کفّه‌یِ حرمان،
کوه
در سنجشِ بی‌هوده‌گی.

□

تو را برگزیده‌ام
رَغماَرَغمِ بی‌داد.
گفتی دوست‌ات می‌دارم
و قاعده
دیگر شد.

کفایت مکن ای فرمانِ «شدن»،
مکرّر شو
مکرّر شو!

۱۷ مردادِ ۱۳۵۹

Nocturnal (No, I Haven't Carved You)

No
I haven't carved you out of my longings—
older than stone,
finer than a new blade of grass.

I haven't forged you out of my rage—
reason
       unable to rise,
flames bursting
            in the furnace of unrest.

I haven't measured you by the weight of my sorrow—
a blade of straw
       on the scale of loss,
a mountain
       as a measure of futility.

☐

I've chosen you
despite the injustice.
You said *I love you*
and the norms
       changed.

Do not relent, O force that commands, "Be," and it becomes!
Repeat yourself,
again and again!

August 8, 1980

در لحظه

به تو دست می‌سایم و جهان را در می‌یابم،
به تو می‌اندیشم
و زمان را لمس می‌کنم
معلق و بی‌انتها
عُریان.

می‌وزم، می‌بارم، می‌تابم.
آسمان‌ام
ستاره‌گان و زمین،
و گندمِ عطرآگینی که دانه می‌بندد
رقصان
در جانِ سبزِ خویش.

◻

از تو عبور می‌کنم
چنان که تُندری از شب. ـ

می‌درخشم
و فرومی‌ریزم.

۱۹ مردادِ ۱۳۵۹

In the Moment

I caress you and discover the world
I think of you
and touch time,
suspended and boundless,
naked.

I blow, I rain, I shine.
I am the sky
the stars and the earth
and the fragrant wheat that sprouts,
dancing
within its green soul.

☐

I pass through you
as thunder through the night—

I glow
and implode.

August 10, 1980

عاشقانه (بیتوته‌ی کوتاهی‌ست جهان)

بیتوته‌ی کوتاهی‌ست جهان
در فاصله‌ی گناه و دوزخ
خورشید
هم‌چون دشنامی برمی‌آید
و روز
شرم‌ساری‌ی جبران‌ناپذیری‌ست.

آه
پیش از آن که در اشک غرقه شوم
چیزی بگوی

درخت،
جهلِ معصیت‌بارِ نیاکان است
و نسیم
وسوسه‌ئی‌ست نابه‌کار.
مهتابِ پائیزی
کفری‌ست که جهان را می‌آلاید.

چیزی بگوی
پیش از آن که در اشک غرقه شوم
چیزی بگوی

هر دریچه‌ی نغز
بر چشم‌اندازِ عقوبتی می‌گشاید.
عشق
رطوبتِ چندش‌انگیزِ پلشتی‌ست
و آسمان
سرپناهی
تا به خاک بنشینی و
بر سرنوشتِ خویش
گریه ساز کنی.

Tenderly (The World is an All-too-brief Way Station)

The world is an all-too-brief way station
                                  between sin and hell
The sun rises
           like a curse
The day,
irreparable disgrace.

Ah
Before I drown in tears
Say something

The tree,
ancestral ignorance, heavy with sin.
The breeze,
           a wicked temptation.
The autumn moonlight,
blasphemy that taints the world.

Say something
Before I drown in tears
           Say something

Every fine portal
opens onto a field of torment
Love—
          scum, damp and vile.
The sky—
          a shelter,
a place on the earth to sit
                    and lament
                            your fate.

آه
پیش از آن که در اشک غرقه شوم چیزی بگوی،
هر چه باشد

چشمه‌ها
از تابوت می‌جوشند
و سوگوارانِ ژولیده آب‌رویِ جهان‌اند.
عصمت به آینه مفروش
که فاجران نیازمندتران‌اند.

خامُش منشین
خدا را
پیش از آن که در اشک غرقه شوم
از عشق
چیزی بگوی!

۲۳ مردادِ ۱۳۵۹

Ah
Say something before I drown in tears
Whatever it may be

Springs well up from coffins,
and disheveled mourners
are the true dignity of the world.
Why cast virtue in the mirror
when the fallen need it more?

Don't stay silent
               For god's sake
Before I drown in tears
Say something
             of love!

    August 14, 1980

مدایحِ بی صله
۱۳۷۱

Unrewarded Eulogies

1992

نمی‌توانم زیبا نباشم...

نمی‌توانم زیبا نباشم
عشوه‌ئی نباشم در تجلی‌یِ جاودانه.

چنان زیبای‌ام من
که گذرگاه‌ام را بهاری نابه‌خویش آذین می‌کند:
در جهانِ پیرامن‌ام
هرگز
خون
عُریانی‌یِ جان نیست
و کبک را
هراس‌ناکی‌یِ سُرب
از خرام
باز
نمی‌دارد.

چنان زیبای‌ام من
که اللهُ‌اکبر
وصفی‌ست ناگزیر
که از من می‌کنی.
زهری بی‌پادزهرم در معرضِ تو.
جهان اگر زیباست
مجیزِ حضورِ مرا می‌گوید. –

ابلها مردا
عدوی‌ِ تو نیستم من
انکارِ توأَم.

۱۳۶۲

I Can't Help But Be Beautiful

I can't help but be beautiful,
a flirtation in eternal light.

I'm so beautiful
that spring spontaneously bursts into bloom in my wake:
in my world
blood
      is never the spirit laid bare
and the fear of lead
           doesn't deter the partridge
from its strut.

I'm so beautiful
that *Allah O Akbar, God is Great*
           can only describe me
I'm venom before you, a poison with no cure.
If the world is beautiful,
it's only because it sings of me—

You imbecile, you,
I'm not your rival
I'm your very denial.

    1983

نمی‌خواستم...

نمی‌خواستم نامِ چنگیز را بدانم
نمی‌خواستم نامِ نادر را بدانم
نامِ شاهان را
محمدِ خواجه و تیمورِ لنگ،
نامِ خِفَّت‌دهندگان را نمی‌خواستم و
خِفَّت‌چشندگان را.

می‌خواستم نامِ تو را بدانم.

و تنها نامی را که می‌خواستم
ندانستم.

۱۳۶۳

I Didn't Want To

I didn't want to know Genghis Khan's name
I didn't want to know Nader Shah's name,
the names of kings—
Mohammad the Eunuch, Timur the Lame
I didn't want the names of tyrants
or of the tyrannized.

I wanted to know your name—

and the only name I wanted was the one
I didn't know.

1984

در جدال با خاموشی

۱

من **بامدادم** سرانجام
خسته
بی آن که جز با خویشتن به جنگ برخاسته باشم.
هرچند جنگی از این فرساینده‌تر نیست،
که پیش از آن که باره برانگیزی
    آگاهی
که سایه‌ی عظیمِ کرکسی گشوده‌بال
بر سراسرِ میدان گذشته است
تقدیرِ از تو گُدازی خون‌آلوده به خاک اندر کرده است
و تو را دیگر
    از شکست و مرگ
گزیر
نیست.

من **بامدادم**
شهروندی با اندام و هوشی متوسط.
نَسَب‌ام با یک حلقه به آواره‌گانِ **کابل** می‌پیوندد.
نامِ کوچک‌ام عربی‌ست
    نامِ قبیله‌ئی‌ام تُرکی
        کُنیَت‌ام پارسی.

نامِ قبیله‌ئی‌ام شرمسارِ تاریخ است
و نامِ کوچک‌ام را دوست نمی‌دارم
(تنها هنگامی که تواَم آواز می‌دهی
این نام زیباترین کلامِ جهان است
و آن صدا غم‌ناک‌ترین آوازِ استمداد).

در شبِ سنگین برفی بی‌امان
بدین رُباط فرودَ آمدم
هم از نخست پیرانه خسته.

Grappling with Silence

1

I am Daybreak, after all,
tired,
      having waged war on no one but myself.
But no war is more grueling
                than knowing—
as you brace for battle—
that the great shadow of a vulture's wings
has already swept
over the battlefield,
that fate has buried
a bloodied voodoo doll of you,
and now
there is no escape
         from death and defeat.

I am Daybreak,
a citizen of average height and wit,
one link removed from the wanderers of Kabul.
My given name—Arabic,
my tribal—Turkic,
my byname—Persian.
My tribal name—the great shame of history.
My given name—I dislike,
    except when you call it.
    Then, it becomes the most beautiful word in the world,
    and that voice, the saddest cry for help.

I landed in this guesthouse of the world
on a relentless night of heavy snow,
already old, already spent.

در خانه‌ئی دل‌گیر انتظارِ مرا می‌کشیدند
کنارِ سقاخانه‌ی آینه
نزدیکِ خانقاهِ درویشان.
(بدین سبب است شاید
که سایه‌ی ابلیس را
هم از اول
همواره در کمینِ خود یافته‌ام).

در پنج‌سالگی
هنوز از ضربه‌ی ناباورِ میلادِ خویش پریشان بودم
و با شغشغه‌ی لوکِ مست و حضورِ ارواحی‌ی خزنده‌گانِ زهرآگین زهرآگین برمی‌بالیدم
بی‌ریشه
بر خاکی شور
در برهوتی دورافتاده‌تر از خاطره‌ی غبارآلودِ آخرین رشته‌ی نخل‌ها بر حاشیه‌ی آخرین خُشک‌رود.

در پنج‌سالگی
بادیه در کف
در ریگ‌زارِ عُریان به دنبالِ نقشِ سراب می‌دویدم
پیشاپیشِ خواهرم که هنوز
با جذبه‌ی کهربائی‌ی مرد
بیگانه بود.

نخستین‌بار که در برابرِ چشمانم **هابیل** مغموم از خویشتن تازیانه خورد
شش‌ساله بودم.
و تشریفات
سخت درخور بود:
صفِ سربازان بود با آرایشِ خاموشِ پیاده‌گانِ سردِ شطرنج،
و شکوهِ پرچمِ رنگین‌رقص
و داردارِ شیپور و رُپ‌رُپه‌ی فرصت‌سوزِ طبل
تا **هابیل** از شنیدنِ زاری‌ی خویش زردروئی نبرد.

They waited for me in a bleak house
by the sacred mirrored fountain
near the mystics' shrine—
      maybe that's why,
      from the start,
      I sensed the shadow of Satan
      lying in wait for me.

At age five
still reeling from the unthinkable blow of my own birth
I grew up
rootless
on salty sand
to the grunting of a drunken camel, to the ghostly presence of venomous snakes,
in a dust bowl
more distant than the fading memory of the last date palms at the edge of a vanished river.

At age five
with an empty bowl in hand
I ran through the naked dunes chasing illusions
ahead of my sister—
still untouched
by the amber allure of men.

When I first laid eyes on grief-stricken Abel flogging himself
                              I was six.
The ceremonies were quite fitting:
A rank of soldiers, a silent parade of cold chess pawns,
a vibrant flag, rippling in splendor,
the blare of trumpets and the merciless pounding of drums—
all to keep Abel from paling at the sound of his own sobbing.

بامدادم من
خسته از با خویشِ جنگیدن
خسته‌یِ سقاخانه و خانقاه و سراب
خسته‌یِ کویر و تازیانه و تحمیل
خسته‌یِ خجلت از خود بردنِ **هابیل**.
دیری‌ست تا دَم بر نیاورده‌ام اما اکنون
هنگامِ آن است که از جگر فریادی برآرم
که سرانجام اینک شیطان که بر من دست می‌گشاید.

صفِ پیادگانِ سرد آراسته است
و پرچم
با هیبتِ رنگین
برافراشته.

تشریفات در ذُروه‌یِ کمال است و بی‌نقصی
راست در خورِ انسانی که برآن‌اند
تا هم‌چون فتیله‌یِ پُردودِ شمعی بی‌بها
به مقراض‌اش بچینند.

در برابرِ صفِ سردَم واداشته‌اند
و دهان‌بندِ زردوز آماده است
بر سینی‌یِ حلبی
کنارِ دسته‌ئی ریحان و پیازی مُشت‌کوب.

آنک نشمه‌یِ نایب که پیش می‌آید عُریان
با خالِ پُرکِرشمه‌یِ اَنگِ وطن بر شرمگاه‌اش
وینک رُپ‌رُپه‌یِ طبل:
تشریفات آغاز می‌شود

هنگامِ آن است که تمامتِ نفرت‌ام را به نعره‌ای بی‌پایان تُف کنم.
من **بامدادِ** نخستین و آخرین‌ام
هابیل‌ام من
بر سکّویِ تحقیر

☐

I am Daybreak,
tired of warring with myself
tired of the fountain, the shrine, the mirage
tired of the desert, the floggings, the burden
tired of Abel's shame of himself.
For too long, I've been silent, but now
I must wrench a cry from the depths of my soul
because at last, the devil has come to claim me.

The rank of infantry stands in formation, cold as stone,
and the flag,
        majestic and vibrant
                flies at full-mast.

The ceremonies are at peak perfection,
befitting the person
to be snipped like the smoking wick
of a worthless candle.

They've stationed me before their cold rank.
The gold-stitched gag is set
on a tin tray
beside a handful of bazaari basil and a smashed onion.

Here comes the lieutenant's mistress, naked,
the seductive mark of the nation's brand on her loins.
Next, the rat-a-tat of drums—
and now, the ceremonies begin.

It's time to spit out my hatred in an endless howl.
I am the first and last Daybreak
I am Abel, upon the stage of disgrace,
the honor of the universe, flogged by my own hand,

شرفِ کیهان‌ام من
تازیانه‌خورده‌ی خویش
که آتشِ سیاهِ اندوه‌ام
دوزخ را
از بضاعتِ ناچیزش شرم‌سار می‌کند.

۲

در بیمارستانی که بسترِ من در آن به جزیره‌ئی در بی‌کرانه‌گی می‌مانَد
گیج و حیرت‌زده به هر سوئی چشم می‌گردانم:

این بیمارستان از آنِ خنازیریان نیست.
سلاطونیان و زنانِ پرستارش لازم و ملزومِ عشرتی بی‌نشاط‌اند.
جذامیان آزادانه می‌خرامند، با پلک‌هایِ نیم‌جویده
و دو قلب در کیسه‌ی فتق
و چرکابه‌ئی از شاش و خاکشی در رگ
با جاروهایِ پَر بر سرنیزه‌ها
به گردگیریِ ویرانه.

راهروها با احساسِ سهم‌گینِ حضورِ سایه‌ئی هیولا که فرمانِ سکوت می‌دهد
محورِ خوابگاه‌هائی‌ست با حَلقه‌هایِ آهن در دیوارهایِ سنگ
و تازیانه و شمشیر بر دیوار.
اسهالیان
شرم را در باغچه‌هایِ پُرگُل به کناره می‌کشند
و قلبِ عافیت در اتاقِ عمل می‌تپد
در تشتکِ خلاب و پنبه
میانِ خُرناسه‌ی کفتارها زیرِ میزِ جراح.

این‌جا قلبِ سالم را زالو تجویز می‌کنند
تا سرخوش و شاد هم‌چون قناریِ مستی
به شیرین‌ترین ترانه‌ی جانات نغمه سردهی تا آستانِ مرگ
که می‌دانی
امنیت
بلالِ شیردانه‌ئی‌ست
که در قفس به نصیب می‌رسد،

and the black fire of my grief
out-shames hell for its measly riches.

2

In the hospital where my bed feels like an island in the infinite,
stunned and bewildered, I scan every direction.

This is no tuberculosis ward.
Cancer patients and their nurses are locked in joyless routines.
Lepers roam freely with half-gnawed eyelids
and two hearts sagging in a hernial sac.
Piss and filth fester in their veins,
as they sweep the ruins
with feathered spears.

The hallways, heavy with a monstrous shadow commanding silence,
form the hub of dormitories, their stone walls lined with metal rings,
whips, and swords.
The diarrhea-stricken
hang their shame on butcher's hooks in flower beds.
The heart of health beats
in a tub of plasma and gauze
in the operating room
while vultures snore under the surgeon's table.

Here, they prescribe leeches for healthy hearts,
so you,
giddy as a drunken canary,
sing the sweetest song of your life right up to the brink of death.
After all, you know that
safety is nothing but porridge
       a reward only granted in a cage—
where the sergeant major
slips into the pocket of your gown

تا استوارِ پاس‌دارخانه برگِ امان در کَفّات نهد
و قوطی‌یِ مُسکن‌ها را در جیبِ روپوش‌ات:
— یکی صبح یکی شب، با عشق!

□

اکنون شبِ خسته از پناهِ شمشادها می‌گذرد
و در آش‌پزخانه
هم‌اکنون
دست‌یارِ جراح
برایِ صبحانه‌یِ سرپزشک
شاعری گردن‌کش را عریان می‌کند
(کسی را اعتراضی هست؟)

و در نعش‌کشی که به گورستان می‌رود
مردگانِ رسمی هنوز تقلائی دارند
و نبض‌ها و زبان‌ها را هنوز
از تبِ خشم کوبش و آتشی هست.

□

عُریان بر میزِ عمل چاربندم
اما باید نعره‌ای برکشم
شرفِ کیهان‌ام آخر
هابیل‌ام من
و در کدوکاسه‌یِ جمجمه‌ام
چاشتِ سرپزشک را نواله‌ئی هست.

به غریوی تلخ
نواله را به کام‌اش زهرِ افعی خواهم کرد،
بامدادم آخر
طلیعه‌یِ آفتاب‌ام.

۲۰ تیرِ ۱۳۶۳

papers of immunity
and a bottle of painkillers:
"*One in the morning, one at night—with love!*"

☐

Now the tired night drifts past the sanctuary of boxwoods
while in the kitchen,
      at this very moment,
the surgeon's assistant
strips an unruly poet naked
to feed the head surgeon for breakfast
(anyone object?)

In the hearse to the graveyard,
the named dead still fight,
their pulses and tongues
pounding with flames of fury.

☐

Naked on the operating table
strapped down by all fours
I must let out a howl—
I am the dignity of the universe, after all
I am Abel
and in the basin of my skull
sits a morsel for the head surgeon's breakfast.

With a bitter cry,
I will turn that morsel into a mouthful of viper's venom.
I am Daybreak, after all—
vanguard of the sun.

  July 11, 1984

جخ امروز از مادر نزاده‌ام...

جخ امروز
از مادر نزاده‌ام
نه
عمرِ جهان بر من گذشته است.

نزدیک‌ترین خاطره‌ام خاطره‌ی قرن‌هاست.
بارها به خون‌مان کشیدند
به یاد آر،
و تنها دست‌آوردِ کشتار
نان‌پاره‌ی بی‌قاتقِ سفره‌ی بی‌برکتِ ما بود.

اعراب فریب‌ام دادند
بُرج موریانه را به دستانِ پُرپینه‌ی خویش بر ایشان در گشودم،
مرا و همه‌گان را بر نطعِ سیاه نشاندند و
گردن زدند.

نماز گزاردم و قتلِ عام شدم
که رافضی‌ام دانستند.
نماز گزاردم و قتلِ عام شدم
که قِرمَطی‌ام دانستند.
آن‌گاه قرار نهادند که ما و برادران‌مان یک‌دیگر را بکشیم و این
کوتاه‌ترین طریقِ وصولِ به بهشت بود!

به یاد آر
که تنها دست‌آوردِ کشتار
جُل‌پاره‌ی بی‌قدرِ عورتِ ما بود.

خوش‌بینی‌ی برادرت تُرکان را آواز داد
تو را و مرا گردن زدند.
سفاهتِ من چنگیزیان را آواز داد
تو را و همه‌گان را گردن زدند.
یوغِ وَرزاو بر گردن‌مان نهادند.

I Wasn't Born Yesterday

I wasn't born yesterday
of a mother,
        no—
the ages of the world have passed through me.

My nearest memories date back centuries.
Many times, they spilled our blood,
remember,
and all we got from the slaughter
were crumbs on our meager spread.

The Arabs tricked me—
with my own calloused hands, I welcomed them into the termite tower.
They sat us on black leather execution mats
and beheaded us.

I turned to prayer, and they slaughtered me
                              branding me a dissenting Rafidi
I turned to prayer, and they slaughtered me
                              branding me a Qarmatian rebel.
Then they preached—brother shalt kill brother,
for this was the shortest road to paradise!

Remember,
all we got from the slaughter
was a tattered scrap to cover our shame.

Your brother's hope summoned the Turks
who beheaded you and me.
My foolishness summoned the Mongols
who beheaded us all.
They yoked us like oxen,
bound us to the plow,

گاوآهن بر ما بستند
بر گُرده‌مان نشستند
و گورستانی چندان بی‌مرز شیار کردند
که بازماندگان را
     هنوز از چشم
         خونابه روان است.

کـــوچ غریب را به یاد آر
از غُربتی به غُربتِ دیگر،
تا جُست‌وجویِ ایمان
    تنها فضیلتِ ما باشد.
به یاد آر:
تاریخ ما بی‌قراری بود
نه باوَری
نه وطنی.

□

نه،
جخ امروز
   از مادر
      نزاده‌ام.

۱۳۶۳

rode our backs
and dug a graveyard so vast
    that survivors still cry
        tears of blood.

Remember how we wandered
from one exile to another,
left with no virtue
but the search for faith.

Remember:
ours was a history of unease—
not of creed
not of country.

  ☐

No,
I wasn't born
    of a mother
       yesterday.

  1984

پس آنگاه زمین...

به شاهرخ جنابیان

پس آنگاه زمین به سخن درآمد
و آدمی، خسته و تنها و اندیشناک بر سر سنگی نشسته بود پشیمان از کرد و کارِ خویش
و زمین به سخن درآمده با او چنین می‌گفت:
ـ به تو نان دادم من، و علف به گوسفندان و به گاوانِ تو، و برگ‌هایِ نازکِ تَرّه که قاتق نان کنی.
انسان گفت: ـ می‌دانم.
پس زمین گفت: ـ به هر گونه صدا من با تو به سخن در آمدم: با نسیم و باد، و با جوشیدنِ چشمه‌ها از سنگ، و با ریزش آبشاران؛ و با فروغلتیدنِ بهمنان از کوه آنگاه که سخت بی‌خبرت می‌یافتم، و به کوسِ تُندر و ترقه‌ی توفان.
انسان گفت: ـ می‌دانم می‌دانم، اما چه‌گونه می‌توانستم رازِ پیامِ تو را دریابم؟
پس زمین با او، با انسان، چنین گفت:
ـ نه خود این سهل بود، که پیام‌گزاران نیز اندک نبودند.
تو می‌دانستی که مَنات به پرستنده‌گی عاشقم‌ام. نیز نه به گونه‌ی عاشقی بختیار، که زرخریده‌وار کنیزککی برای تو بودم به رایِ خویش. که تو را چندان دوست می‌داشتم که چون دست بر من می‌گشودی تن و جانام به هزار نغمه‌ی خوش جواب‌گوی تو می‌شد. هم‌چون نوعروسی در رختِ زفاف، که ناله‌های تن‌آزردگی‌اش به ترانه‌ی کشف و کامیاری بدل شود یا چنگی که هر زخمه را به زیر و بَمی دل‌پذیر دیگرگونه جوابی گوید. ـ آی، چه عروسی، که هر بار سربه‌مُهر با بسترِ تو درآمد! (چنین می‌گفت زمین.) در کدامین بادیه چاهی کردی که به آبی گوارا کامیاب‌ات نکردم؟ کجا به دستانِ خشونت‌باری که انتظار سوزانِ نوازش حاصل‌خیزش با من است گاوآهن در من نهادی که خرمنی پُربار پاداش ندادم؟
انسان دیگرباره گفت: ـ رازِ پیامات را اما چه‌گونه می‌توانستم دریابم؟
ـ می‌دانستی که مَنات عاشقانه دوست می‌دارم (زمین به پاسخ او چنین گفت). می‌دانستی. و تو را پس پیغام کردم از پس پیغام به هزار آوا، که دل از آسمان بردار که وحی از خاک می‌رسد. پیغامات کردم از پسِ پیغام که مقامِ تو جای‌گاهِ بنده‌گان نیست، که در این گستره شهریاری تو؛ و آن‌چه تو را به شهریاری برداشت نه عنایتِ آسمان که مهرِ زمین است.
ـ آه که مرا در آن مرتبتِ خاک‌ساری‌یِ عاشقانه، بر گستره‌یِ نامتناهی‌یِ

And Then the Earth...

To Shahrokh Jenabian

Then the earth spoke and man, tired, alone, and lost in thought, sat upon a rock, remorseful for his deeds.

The earth said to him:
— I gave you bread, grass for your cattle, and tender leaves of leek to season your bread.

— I know, said man.

The earth continued:
— I spoke to you in every voice: the breeze and the wind, springs gushing from rocks, waterfalls cascading, avalanches crashing down the mountains. When I found you utterly unaware, I spoke in thunder's clap, in the storm's crack.

— I know, said man. I know, but how could I have grasped the secret of your message?

Then the earth told man:
— It was no easy feat, and the messengers were not few. You knew I worshiped you with the devotion of a lover—not a fortunate one, but like a servant girl bought with gold, willingly offering herself. My love for you ran so deep that every touch of yours stirred a thousand sweet songs in my body and soul—like a bride on her wedding night, her cries of pain turning into songs of discovery and joy, or like a harp responding to each pluck with a new, pleasing tone.

Ah, what a bride I was! Time and again, I came to your bed untouched! In which desert did you dig a well that I did not reward you with cool waters? Where, with your harsh hands, whose fruitful, burning caress I yearned for, did you drive your plow into me without my giving you a bountiful harvest?

کیهانِ خوشِ سلطنتی بود، که سرسبز و آباد از قدرت‌هایِ جادوئی‌یِ تو بودم از آن پیش که تو پادشاهِ جانِ من به خربنده‌گی‌یِ آسمانْ دست‌ها بر سینه و پیشانی به خاک برنهی و مرا چنین به خواری درافکنی.

انسان، اندیش‌ناک و خسته و شرمسار، از ژرفاهای درد ناله‌ئی کرد. و زمین، هم از آن‌گونه در سخن بود:
ـ به تمامی از آنِ تو بودم و تسلیمِ تو، چون چاردیواری‌یِ خانه‌یِ کوچکی. تو را عشقِ من آن مایه توانائی داد که بر همه سَر شَوی. دریغا، پنداری گناه من همه آن بود که زیرِ پایِ تو بودم!
تا از خونِ من پرورده شَوی به دردمندی دندان بر جگر فشردم هم‌چون مادری که دردِ مکیده شدن را تا نوزاده‌یِ دامنِ خود را از عصاره‌یِ جانِ خویش نوشاکی دهد.
تو را آموختم من که به جُست‌وجویِ سنگِ آهن و روی، سینه‌یِ عاشقانم را بردری. و این همه از برایِ آن بود تا تو را در نوازشِ پُرخشونتی که از دستانت چشم داشتم دست‌افزاری به دست داده باشم. اما تو روی از من برتافتی، که آهن و مس را از سنگ‌پاره کُشنده‌تر یافتی که **هابیل** را در خون کشیده بود. و خاک را از قربانیانِ بدکنشی‌هایِ خویش بارور کردی.
آه، زمینْ تنها مانده! زمین رها شده با تنهائی‌یِ خویش!
انسان زیرِ لب گفت: ـ تَقدیر چنین بود. مگر آسمان قربانی‌ئی می‌خواست.

ـ نه، که مرا گورستانی می‌خواهد! (چنین گفت زمین).
و تو بی‌احساسِ عمیقِ سرشکسته‌گی چه‌گونه از «تقدیر» سخن می‌گوئی که جز بهانه‌یِ تسلیمِ بی‌همتان نیست؟
آن افسون‌کار به تو می‌آموزد که عدالت از عشق والاتر است. ـ دریغا که اگر عشق به کار می‌بود هرگز ستمی در وجود نمی‌آمد تا به عدالتی نابه‌کارانه از آن دست نیازی پدید افتد. ـ آن‌گاه چشمانِ تو را بربسته شمشیری در کَفات می‌گذارد، هم از آهنی که من به تو دادم تا تیغه‌یِ گاوآهن کنی!
اینک گورستانی که آسمان از عدالت ساخته است!
دریغا ویرانِ بی‌حاصلی که منم!

□

شب و باران در ویرانه‌ها به گفت‌وگو بودند که باد دررسید، میانه‌به‌هم‌زن و پُرهیاهو.

— But how could I have grasped the secret of your message? repeated man.

— You knew I loved you! said the earth.
You knew. Message after message, I spoke to you in a thousand voices, urging you to turn away from the heavens, because revelation comes from the earth. Again and again, I told you that your place is not among servants. In this vast expanse, you are the sovereign. And what raised you to sovereignty was not the grace of the heavens, but the love of the earth! Ah, how joyously I reigned over the boundless universe in loving humility. I was lush and thriving with your magical powers long before you, king of my soul, bowed low to the heavens—hands on chest, forehead to the ground—like a mere servant, casting me so miserably into disgrace.

Man groaned, tired, ashamed, lost in thought. And the earth spoke in kind:
— I was wholly yours, surrendered like the four walls of a humble home. It was my love for you that gave you the strength to rise above all else. Alas, my only sin was being beneath your feet! I endured the agony, gritting my teeth to nourish you with my blood, like a mother drained to feed her newborn with the essence of her life.

I taught you to tear open my loving chest in search of iron and zinc, arming you for the cruel touch I had come to expect from your hands. Yet you turned your back on me, wielding iron and copper, deadlier than the stone that spilled Abel's blood. You fertilized the earth with the victims of your misdeeds.

O, forsaken earth! Earth abandoned to its solitude!

— So it was. Maybe the heavens demanded a sacrifice, man muttered.

— No! The heavens wish me to be a graveyard! said the earth.
How can you speak of "fate" without shame, knowing it is nothing but a pretext for the cowardly to surrender?

دیری نگذشت که خلاف در ایشان افتاد و غوغا بالا گرفت بر سراسرِ خاک، و به خاموش‌باش‌هایِ پُرغریوِ تُندر حرمت نگذاشتند.

□

زمین گفت: – اکنون به دوراهه‌یِ تفریق رسیده‌ایم.
تو را جز زردروئی کشیدن از بی‌حاصلی‌یِ خویش گزیر نیست؛ پس اکنون که به تقدیرِ فریبکار گردن نهاده‌ای مردانه باش!
اما مرا که ویرانِ توام هنوز در این مدارِ سردِ کار به پایان نرسیده است:
هم‌چون زنی عاشـق که به بسترِ معشوقِ از دسـت رفته‌یِ خویش می‌خزد تا بویِ او را دریابد، سال همه سال به مُقامِ نخستین باز می‌آیم با اشک‌هایِ خاطره.
یـادِ بهـاران بر مـن فرود می‌آیـد بی‌آن‌که از شـخمی تـازه بار برگرفته باشـم و گسترشِ ریشـه‌ئی را در بطنِ خود احساس کنم؛ و ابرها با خس و خاری کـه در آغوش‌ام خواهند نهَاد، با اشـک‌هایِ عقیـمِ خویش به تسلای‌ام خواهند کوشید.
جانِ مرا اما تسلائی مقدر نیست:
به غیـابِ دردناکِ تو سـلطانِ شکسـته‌یِ کهکشـان‌ها خواهم اندیشـید که به افسونِ پلیدی از پای درآمدی؛

و ردِّ انگشتانات را
بر تنِ نومیدِ خویش
در خاطره‌ئی گریان
جُست‌وجو
خواهم کرد.

تابستان‌هایِ ۱۳۴۳ و ۱۳۶۳

That sorcerer teaches you that justice is prized over love. But if love had reigned, no injustice would have existed to breed this twisted justice. Then, blindfolding you, he places a sword in your hand, cast from the very iron I gave you to forge a plowshare!

Behold the graveyard the heavens built in the name of justice!
Alas, the barren ruin I have become!

☐

Night and rain were talking among the ruins when wind arrived—raucous and unruly. Discord erupted, chaos spread across the land, defying thunder's command for silence.

☐

The earth spoke: — Now, we stand at the crossroads of division.
You must bear the shame of your own futility. If you've bowed to deceitful fate, then face it like a man!

As for me, the ruin you have made of me, my task in this cold orbit is far from complete: like a lover slipping into her long-lost beloved's bed to catch his lingering scent, I return, year after year, to my source, weeping in remembrance.

Spring's memory washes over me, yet I yield no harvest from a new plow and feel no roots take hold in me. The clouds will cradle me in thorns and debris, offering their barren tears as consolation.
But I cannot be consoled.
I will dwell on your painful absence, vanquished sovereign of the galaxies, undone by an evil spell!

And upon my despairing body,
I will seek
>   the trace
>   of your fingers
>   in a memory
>   steeped in tears.

The summers of 1964 and 1984

دوست‌ات می‌دارم بی...

دوست‌ات می‌دارم بی‌آن‌که بخواهم‌ات.

□

سال‌گشته‌گی‌ست این
که به خود درپیچی ابروار
بِغُرّی بی‌آن‌که بباری؟

سال‌گشته‌گی‌ست این
که بخواهی‌اش
بی‌این که بیفشاری‌اش؟

سال‌گشته‌گی‌ست این؟
خواستن‌اش
تمنای هر رگ
بی‌آن‌که در میان باشد
خواهشی حتا؟

نهایتِ عاشقی‌ست این؟
آن وعده‌ی دیدار در فراسویِ پیکرها؟

۲۲ خردادِ ۱۳۶۷

I Love You Without…

I love you without wanting you.

    ☐

Is it old age
to coil inward like a cloud
and thunder without rain?

Is it old age
to want her
without clasping her?

Is it old age
to want her,
ache for her in every vein
without even
a single plea?

Is this the pinnacle of love,
the promise of union beyond the body?

June 11, 1988

نِلسن ماندِلا

تو آن سویِ زمینی در قفسِ سوزانات
من این سوی:
و خطِ رابطِ ما فارغ از شایبه‌ی زمان است
کوتاه‌ترین فاصله‌ی جهان است.

زی من به اعتماد دستی دراز کن
ای هم‌سایه‌ی درد.

مَرَدَنگی‌ی شمعی لرزانی تو در وقاحتِ باد،
خُنیاگرِ مدیحی از یاد رفته‌ایم ما
در اُرجوزه‌ی وَهن.

نه تو تنها
خوش‌نشینِ نُه‌توی ایثاری
که عاشقان
همه
خویشاوندان‌اند
تا بیگانه نه انگاری.

با ما به اعتماد سرودی ساز کن
ای هم‌سایه‌ی درد.

بهمنِ ۱۳۶۷

Nelson Mandela

You are on that side of the world in your burning cage,
and I am on this side—
but the line connecting us is untainted by time,
the shortest distance in the world.

        Extend a hand in faith toward me,
        Oh you, neighbor in pain.

You shield the flickering flame against the brazen wind.
We are minstrels of forgotten praises
                in the battle-cry of taunts.

You are not alone
        in the nine folds of self-sacrifice—
all lovers are kin,
        don't count them
as strangers.

        Sing us a song in trust,
        Oh you, neighbor in pain.

February 1989

ای کاش آب بودم...

به مفتون امینی
وسواسِ مهربانِ شعر

ای کاش آب بودم
گر می‌شد آن باشی که خود می‌خواهی. -
آدمی بودن
حسرتا!
مشکلی‌ست در مرزِ ناممکن. نمی‌بینی؟

ای کاش آب بودم - به خود می‌گویم -
نهالی نازک به درختی گَشن رساندن را
(- تا به زخمِ تبر بر خاک‌اش افکنند
در آتش سوختن را؟)
یا نشایِ سستِ کاجی را سرسبزیِ جاودانه بخشیدن
(- از آن پیش‌تر که صلیبی‌ش آلوده کنند
به لختهٔ لختهٔ خونی بی‌حاصل؟)

یا به سیراب کردنِ لب تشنه‌ئی
رضایتِ خاطری احساس کردن
(- حتا اگرش به زانو نشانده‌اند
در میدانی جوشان از آفتاب و عربده
تا به شمشیری گردن‌اش بزنند؟
حیرتات را برنمی‌انگیزد
قابیل برادرِ خود شدن
یا جلّادِ دیگراندیشان؟
یا درختی بالیده نابالیده را
حتا
هیمه‌ئی انگاشتنِ بی‌جان؟)

□

می‌دانم می‌دانم می‌دانم
با این همه کاش ای کاش آب می‌بودم
گر توانستمی آن باشم که دل‌خواهِ من است.

I Wish I Were Water...

> To Maftoon Amini
> The gentle obsession of poetry

I wish I were water—
if only you could be what you long to be.
Ah, being human—
    a struggle teetering on the edge of the impossible, don't you see?

I tell myself, I wish I were water,
to nurture a tender sapling into a mighty tree—
    (only to see it felled by an ax's blow,
    thrown into the flames?)
or to bring eternal green to a fragile sprouting pine—
    (only for it to become a cross,
    stained with clots of wasted blood?)
or to feel the satisfaction of quenching parched lips—
    (even if he is forced to kneel
    on a field of blazing sun and raging cries,
    a sword poised at his neck?
    Doesn't it baffle you
    to become Cain, your brother's slayer,
    or to wield the blade against free minds?
                                  Or worse—
    to see a barely grown tree
    as nothing more than lifeless kindling?)

    ☐

I know, I know, I know
Yet still, I wish, oh how I wish, I were water—
if only you could be what you long to be.

آه
کاش هنوز
به بی‌خبری
قطره‌ئی بودم پاک
از نَم‌باری
به کوه‌پایه‌ئی
نه در این اقیانوسِ کشاکشِ بی‌داد
سرگشته موجِ بی‌مایه‌ئی.

۳۰ شهریورِ ۱۳۶۸

Ah,
if only I could remain
a pure drop, unaware,
from a gentle mist
on some quiet mountainside—
not tossed around in this ruthless ocean,
a helpless wave
lost in the chaos.

September 21, 1989

در آستانه
۱۳۷۶

At the Threshold

1997

در آستانه

باید اِستاد و فرود آمد
بر آستانِ دری که کوبه ندارد،
چرا که اگر به‌گاه آمده باشی دربان به انتظارِ توست و
اگر بی‌گاه
به درکوفتن‌ات پاسخی نمی‌آید.

کوتاه است در،
پس آن به که فروتن باشی.
آئینه‌ئی نیک پرداخته توانی بود
آن‌جا
تا آراستگی را
پیش از درآمدن
در خود نظری کنی
هرچند که غلغله‌ی آن سویِ در زاده‌ی توهمِ توست نه انبوهی‌یِ مهمانان،
که آن‌جا
تو را
کسی به انتظار نیست.
که آن‌جا
جنبش شاید،
اما جُمَنده‌ئی در کار نیست:
نه ارواح و نه اشباح و نه قدیسانِ کافورینه به کف
نه عفریتانِ آتشین گاوسر به مشت
نه شیطانِ بُهتان‌خورده با کلاهِ بوقی‌یِ منگوله‌دارش
نه ملغمه‌یِ بی‌قانونِ مطلق‌هایِ مُتنافَی. –
تنها تو
آن‌جا موجودیتِ مطلقی،
موجودیتِ محض،
چرا که در غیابِ خود ادامه می‌یابی و غیابات
حضورِ قاطع اعجاز است.
گذارت از آستانه‌ی ناگزیر
فرو چکیدنِ قطره‌یِ قطرانی‌ست در نامتناهی‌یِ ظلمات:

At the Threshold

One must stop and step down
at the threshold of a door with no knocker—
because if you've arrived in time, the doorkeeper is waiting.
But if you're late,
your knocking will be met with silence.

The door is low,
so best to be humble.
There, you could be a finely polished mirror
to study your reflection before entering—
even if the commotion on the other side
is only a figment of your imagination,
not an actual crowd.

Because there,
no one waits for you.

Because there,
movement may exist,
but no creature to speak of:

no spirits, no phantoms, no saints with camphor-scented hands,
nor fiery, bull-headed demons with clenched fists,
no maligned Satan in his party hat with pompoms,
no random mix of conflicting absolutes.

Only you
are absolute there,
pure being.

You persist in your absence,
and your absence is the surest presence of miracles.

« – دریغا
ای کاش ای کاش
قضاوتی قضاوتی قضاوتی
درکارِ درکارِ درکار
می‌بود!» –

شاید اگرت توانِ شنفتن بود
پژواکِ آوازِ فروچکیدنِ خود را در تالارِ خاموشِ کهکشان‌هایِ بی‌خورشید –
چون هُرَّستِ آوارِ دریغ
می‌شنیدی:
«– کاش‌کی کاش‌کی
داوری داوری داوری
درکارِ درکارِ درکارِ درکار...»
اما داوری آن سویِ در نشسته است، بی‌ردایِ شومِ قاضیان.
ذات‌اش درایت و انصاف
هیأت‌اش زمان. –
و خاطره‌ات تا جاودانِ جاویدان در گذرگاهِ ادوارِ داوری خواهد شد.

□

بدرود!
بدرود! (چنین گوید **بامدادِ** شاعر:)
رقصان می‌گذرم از آستانه‌یِ اجبار
شادمانه و شاکر.

از بیرون به درون آمدم:
از منظر
به نظّاره به ناظر. –
نه به هیأتِ گیاهی نه به هیأتِ پروانه‌ئی نه به هیأتِ سنگی نه به هیأتِ برکه‌ئی، –
من به هیأتِ «ما» زاده شدم
به هیأتِ پُرشکوهِ انسان
تا در بهارِ گیاه به تماشایِ رنگین‌کمانِ پروانه بنشینم
غرورِ کوه را دریابم و هیبتِ دریا را بشنوم
تا شریعتی‌یِ خود را بشناسم و جهان را به قدرِ همت و فرصتِ خویش معنا دهم
که کارستانی از این دست

Your passage through the inevitable threshold
is like droplets trickling into the infinite void:

"Alas,
if only, if only
a judgment, a judgment, a judgment
were in place, in place, in place."

Perhaps if you could listen,
you would hear the echo of your trickling
through the silent hall of sunless galaxies—
a roar, a crash of ruinous regret:

"If only, if only,
a justice, a justice, a justice
were in place, in place, in place, in place…"

But beyond the door, justice sits
without the grim cloak of judges,
its nature wisdom and fairness,
its form time itself.

And your memory shall be judged
eternally and forever
in the cycles of time to come.

  ☐

Farewell!
Farewell!
(So says Bamdad the poet):

I dance across the threshold of duty,
joyous, grateful.

از توانِ درخت و پرنده و صخره و آبشار
بیرون است.

انسان زاده شدن تجسّدِ وظیفه بود:
توانِ دوست داشتن و دوست‌داشته شدن
توانِ شنفتن
توانِ دیدن و گفتن
توانِ اندُه‌گین و شادمان شدن
توانِ خندیدن به وسعتِ دل، توانِ گریستن از سُویدای جان
توانِ گردن به غرور برافراشتن در ارتفاعِ شُکوه‌ناکِ فروتنی
توانِ جلیل به دوش بردنِ بارِ امانت
و توانِ غم‌ناکِ تحملِ تنهائی
تنهائی
تنهائی
تنهائیِ عریان.

انسان
دشواریِ وظیفه است.

□

دستانِ بسته‌ام آزاد نبود تا هر چشم‌انداز را به جان در برکشم
هر نغمه و هر چشمه و هر پرنده
هر بَدرِ کامل و هر پگاهِ دیگر
هر قلّه و هر درخت و هر انسانِ دیگر را.

رخصتِ زیستن را دست بسته دهان بسته گذشتم دست و دهان بسته گذشتیم
و منظرِ جهان را
تنها
از رخنه‌ی تنگ‌چشمیِ حصارِ شرارت دیدیم و
اکنون
آنک دَرِ کوتاهِ بی‌کوبه در برابر و
آنک اشارتِ دربانِ منتظر! ـ

I journeyed from the outside in:
from the sight,
to the seeing,
to the seer—

not as a plant, butterfly, rock, or pond,
but born as *we*,
in the glorious form of the human:

to witness the butterfly's rainbow in the plant's spring
to grasp the mountain's pride
to hear the sea's majesty
to know my own promise
to shape the world's meaning
by the scale of my might and fate.

Because such wonders
lie beyond the reach
of trees and birds and rocks and waterfalls.

To be born human was to embody duty:
to love and be loved
to listen
to see and speak
to grieve and rejoice
to laugh with a full heart
to weep from the depths of the soul
to hold one's head high in noble humility
to bear the Burden of Trust with honor
to endure the aching weight of loneliness—

the loneliness
the loneliness
the naked loneliness.

دالانِ تنگی را که درنوشته‌ام
به وداع
فراپُشت می‌نگرم:

فرصت کوتاه بود و سفر جان‌کاه بود
اما یگانه بود و هیچ کم نداشت.

به جانْ منت‌پذیرم و حق‌گزارم!
(چنین گفت **بامدادِ** خسته.)

۲۹ آبانِ ۱۳۷۱

To be human
is the burden of the duty.

☐

My bound hands were not free
to embrace every scene,
every song, every spring, every bird
every full moon and every new dawn
every peak, every tree, every fellow human.

I lived life with hands tied, mouth shut.
We lived it, hands and mouths bound,
catching glimpses of the world's spectacle
only through the narrow crack
in the prison wall of spite.

And now,
before us looms a low door with no knocker,
a signal from the waiting doorkeeper

I glance back,
a final farewell to the narrow hallway I leave behind

Time was short and the journey grueling.
But it was singular and lacked nothing.

On my soul, I am indebted and grateful!
(So said Bamdad the exhausted.)

November 20, 1992

طبیعتِ بی‌جان

به میترا اسپهبد

دسته‌یِ کاغذ
بر میز
در نخستین نگاهِ آفتاب.

کتابی مبهم و
سیگاری خاکستر شده کنارِ فنجانِ چایِ از یادرفته.

بحثی ممنوع
در ذهن.

آذرِ ۱۳۷۱

Still Life

To Mitra Espahbod

A pile of paper
on the table
in the first glimpse of the sun.

An obscure book and
a burnt-to-ashes cigarette next to the forgotten cup of tea.

A forbidden thought
on the mind.

December 1992

میلاد

ناگهان
عشق
آفتاب‌وار
نقاب برافکند
و بام و در
به صوتِ تجلی
درآکند،
شعشعه‌یِ آذرخش‌وار
فروکاست
و انسان
برخاست.

۵ اردیبهشتِ ۱۳۷۶

Birth

Suddenly
        love appeared
                like the sun
and the heavens
        filled
                with the sound of appearance,
the glare of lightning
            dimmed
and Human
stood tall.

April 25, 1997

حدیثِ بی‌قراریِ ماهان
۱۳۷۹

The Tale of Mahan's Restlessness

2000

آشتی

« – اقیانوس است آن:
ژرفا و بی‌کرانه‌گی،
پرواز و گرداب و خیزاب
بی آن که بداند.

کوه است این:
شُکوهِ پادرجائی،
فراز و فرود و گردن‌کشی
بی این که بداند.

مرا اما
انسان آفریده‌ای:
ذره‌یِ بی‌شکوهی
گدایِ پَشم و پِشکِ جانوران،
تا تو را به خواری تسبیح گوید
از وحشتِ قهرت بر خود بلرزد
بی‌گانه از خود چنگ در تو زند
تا تو
کُل باشی.

مرا انسان آفریده‌ای:
شرمسارِ هر لغزشِ ناگزیرِ تن‌راش
سرگردانِ عرصاتِ دوزخ و سرنگونِ چاه‌سارهایِ عَفِن:
یا خشنودِ گردن نهادن به غلامی‌یِ تو
سرگردانِ باغی بی‌صفا با گل‌هایِ کاغذین.

فانی‌ام آفریده‌ای
پس هرگزت دوستی نخواهد بود که پیمان به آخر برد.

بر خود مبال که اشرفِ آفرینه‌گانِ توأَم من:
با من
خدائی را
شکوهی مقدّر نیست.»

Reconciliation

"That one is an ocean—
all immensity and depth
vortex, tide, and flight—
                without knowing it.

This one is a mountain—
splendor of permanence
ascent, descent, and defiance—
                without knowing it.

Yet you made me human—
                a speck without majesty,
at the mercy of fur and fleece,
to praise you in humility,
                to tremble at your wrath,
estranged from myself,
clawing at you—
                so that you may be whole.

You made me human—
ashamed of every inevitable slip of the flesh,
lost in the infernal fields, plunging into foul pits,
or content to submit to your servitude,
lost in a lifeless garden of paper flowers.

You made me mortal,
so you'll never have a friend who sees the covenant through to the end.

Don't boast that I'm your crowning creation—
to me,
        your godliness falls
                short of glory."

« – نقشِ غلط مخوان
هان!
اقیانوس نیستی تو
جلوه‌ی سیالِ ظلماتِ درون.
کوه نیستی
خشکینه‌یِ بی‌انعطافی‌یِ محض.
انسانی تو
سرمستِ خُمِ فرزانه‌گی‌ئی
که هنوز از آن قطره‌ئی بیش درنکشیده
از مُعماهایِ سیاه سر برآورده
هستی
معنایِ خود را با تو محک می‌زند.

از دوزخ و بهشت و فرش و عرش برمی‌گذری
و دایره‌یِ حضورت
جهان را
در آغوش می‌گیرد.

نامِ توأَم من
به یاوه معنایم مکن!»

فروردینِ ۱۳۶۴

☐

"Don't be fooled by appearances.
                              Listen!

You're not an ocean,
the fluid mirror of inner darkness.
You're not a mountain,
Sheer, motionless rock.
You are human,
drunk on wisdom's cup—
though you've only sipped a drop.
Born of deep mysteries,
existence weighs its worth
                              in you.

You transcend heaven and hell,
                              earth and sky
The sphere of your presence
                              embraces the world.

I am your name—
don't turn me into nothing!"

April 1985

The Day After

در واپسین دم
واپسین خردمندِ غم‌خوارِ حیات
ارابه‌یِ جنگی را تمهیدی کرد
که از دودِ سوختِ رانه و احتراقِ خرجِ سلاح‌اش
اکسیری می‌ساخت
که خاک را بارورتر می‌کرد و
فضا را از آلودگی مانع می‌شد!

۲ بهمنِ ۱۳۷۱

The Day After

With his final breath
the last sage who cherished life
forged a chariot of war
that transformed its fumes and weapon's discharge
into an elixir
fertilizing the soil
and purifying the air!

January 21, 1993

سرودِ ششم

شگفتا
    که نبودیم
        عشقِ ما
            در ما
        حضورِمان داد.
پیوندیم اکنون
    آشنا
چون خنده با لب و اشک با چشم

واقعه‌ی نخستین دمِ ماضی.

       □

غریویم و غوغا
    اکنون،
نه کلامی به مثابهِ مصداقی
که صوتی به نشانه‌ی رازی.

       □

هزار معبد به یکی شهر...

بشنو:
گو یکی باشد معبد به همه دهر
تا من آن‌جا برم نماز
که تو باشی.

چندان دخیل مبند که بخشکانی‌ام از شرمِ ناتوانی‌یِ خویش:
درختِ معجزه نیستم
تنها یکی درخت‌ام
نوجی در آب‌کندی،
و جز این‌ام هنری نیست
که آشیانِ تو باشم،
تختات و
تابوتات.

The Sixth Song

What a wonder
        that we once didn't exist,
that the love inside us
        birthed us.
Now we are one,
intimate—
like a smile to lips, like tears to eyes—

the first moment of our history.

☐

We are all uproar and outcry
        now,
not a word that means,
but a sound that points to a mystery.

☐

To each city a thousand temples…

Listen:
Say there is only one in the whole world
where I go to pray,
where you are.

Don't tie so many threads of hope to the shrine—
you'd shrink me in shame at my own failings:
I am no tree of miracles,
only a tree,
a lone pine in a pool,
with no art but this—
to be your nest,
your seat,
        and sarcophagus.

□
- یادگاریم و خاطره اکنون. –

دو پرنده
یادمانِ پروازی
و گلوئیِ خاموش
یادمانِ آوازی.

۹ فروردینِ ۱۳۷۲

☐
We are memento and memory now—

two birds,
relics of a flight,
and a silent throat,
relic of a song.

March 29, 1993

شب‌بیداران

همه شب حیران‌اش بودم،
حیرانِ شهرِ بیدار
که پی‌سوزِ چشمان‌اش می‌سوخت و
اندیشه‌ی خوابش به سر نبود
و نجوایِ اورادش
لَخت لَخت
آسمانِ سیاه را می‌انباشت
چون لَتِرمَه باتلاقی دمه بوناک
که فضا را.

حیران بودم همه شب
شهرِ بیدار را
که آوازِ دهان‌اش
تنها
همهمه‌ی عَفِنِ اذکارش بود:
شهرِ بی‌خواب
با پی‌سوزِ پُردودِ بیداری‌اش
در شبِ قدری چنان. ـ
در شبِ قدری.

□

گفتم: «بنخفتی، شهر!
همه شب
به نجوا
نگرانِ چه بودی؟»

گفتند:
«برآمدنِ روز را
به دعا
شب‌زنده‌داری کردیم.
مگر به یُمنِ دعا
آفتاب
برآید.»

Those Who Stand Vigil in the Night

All night, I was bewildered by it,
lost in the wakeful city,
its eyes burning like an oil lamp,
sleep never crossing its mind.
The whispers of its prayers
rose into the black sky,
                    bit by bit,
like a bog-born stench
                          thickening the air.

All night, I was bewildered
                    by the wakeful city,
whose mouth sang
            nothing
                    but the foul hum of its vespers:—
the sleepless city
its smokey lamp of wakefulness flickering
on such a Night of Destiny,
on a Night of Destiny.

    ☐

I asked: "City, you haven't slept!
All night,
        whispering—
                what kept you awake?"

They said:
        "We kept vigil
                all night
                      praying for dawn,
hoping that, by the grace of our prayers,
the sun would rise."

گفتم: «حاجتْ‌روا شدید
که آنک سپیده!»

به آهی گفتند: «کنون
به جمعیتِ خاطر
دل به دریای خواب می‌زنیم
که حاجتِ نومیدانه
چنین معجز آیت
برآمد.»

۸ فروردینِ ۱۳۷۳

I said: "Your prayers were answered

                    Look—the dawn!

With a sigh, they said: "Now

                at last, with peace of mind
we plunge into the sea of sleep.
For hopeless as we were,
our prayers have been answered
like a miracle."

March 28, 1994

با تخلصِ خونینِ بامداد

مرگ آن‌گاه پاتابه همی‌گشود که خروسِ سحرگهی
بانگی همه از بلور سر می‌داد –

گوش به بانگِ خروسان در سپردم
هم از لحظه‌ی تُردِ میلادِ خویش.

□

مرگ آن‌گاه پاتابه همی‌گشود که پوپکِ زردخال
بی شانه‌ی نقره به صحرا سر می‌نهاد –

به چشم، تاجی به خاک افگنده جُستم
هم از لحظه‌ی نگرانِ میلادِ خویش.

□

مرگ آن‌گاه پاتابه همی‌گشود که کبکِ خرامان
خنده‌ی غفلت به دامنه سر می‌داد –

به درکشیدنِ جامِ قهقهه همت نهادم
هم از لحظه‌ی گریانِ میلادِ خویش.

□

مرگ آن‌گاه پاتابه همی‌گشود که درختِ بهارپوش
رختِ غبارآلوده به قامت می‌آراست –

چشم به راهِ خزانِ تلخ نشستم
هم از لحظه‌ی نومیدِ میلادِ خویش.

□

مرگ آن‌گاه پاتابه همی‌گشود که هَزارِ سیاه‌پوش
بر شاخسارِ خزانی ترانه‌ی بدرود ساز می‌کرد –

Written in Dawn's Blood

Death was unlacing its boots
when the rooster's call split the crystal dawn—

        I've been listening to the rooster's call
        since the brittle moment of my birth

☐

Death was unlacing its boots
when the yellow-crested hoopoe set out for the plain, without its silver comb—

        I've looked for the fallen crown with my own eyes
        since the watchful moment of my birth

☐

Death was unlacing its boots
when the strutting partridge cast a careless laugh down the hillside—

        I've struggled to down the cup of mirth
        since the tearful moment of my birth

☐

Death was unlacing its boots
when the blooming tree donned its dusty robe—

        I've waited for bitter autumn
        since the dismal moment of my birth

☐

Death was unlacing its boots
when the black-feathered bird sang its farewell song on autumn's branch—

با تخلصِ سُرخ بامداد به پایان بردم
لحظه لحظه‌یِ تلخِ انتظارِ خویش.

۲۷ آذرِ ۱۳۷۶

I ended my wait, moment by bitter moment,
with the crimson pen name of Dawn.

December 18, 1997

نخستین که در جهان دیدم...

به دکتر جهانگیر رأفت

نخستین که در جهان دیدم
از شادی غریو برکشیدم:
«من‌ام، آه
آن معجزتِ نهایی
بر سیاره‌یِ کوچکِ آب و گیاه!»

آن‌گاه که در جهان زیستم
از شگفتی بر خود تپیدم:
میراث‌خوارِ آن سفاهتِ ناباور بودن
که به چشم و به گوش می‌دیدم و می‌شنیدم!

چندان که در پیرامنِ خویشتن دیدم
به ناباوریِ گریه در گلو شکسته بودم:
بنگر چه درشت‌ناک تیغ بر سرِ من آخته
آن که باورِ بی‌دریغ در او بسته بودم.

اکنون که سراچه‌یِ اعجاز پسِ پُشت می‌گذارم
به‌جز آهِ حسرتی با من نیست:
تَبَری غرقه‌یِ خون
بر سکویِ باورِ بی‌یقین و
باریکه‌یِ خونی که از بلندایِ یقین جاری‌ست.

۱۲ اسفندِ ۱۳۷۷

When I First Saw the World...

To Dr. Jahangir Ra'fat

When I first saw the world
I cried in joy:
> *Ah, it's me*
> *that pinnacle of miracles*
> *on the little planet of seas and trees!*

Once I lived in the world,
I shuddered with the shock—
being heir to the unthinkable folly
that I witnessed with my own eyes and ears!

The more I looked around me,
the more I choked back tears of disbelief—
see the brazen ax hoisted above my head
by the one I trusted fully.

Now all I carry is a sigh of regret
as I leave this tower of wonders behind—
a blood-soaked ax
on the pulpit of faithless creed
while a trickle of blood flows from the heights of faith.

March 3, 1999

کژمژ و بی‌انتها...

کژمژ و بی‌انتها
به طولِ زمان‌هایِ پیش و پس
ستونِ استخوان‌ها
چشم‌خانه‌ها تهی
دنده‌ها عریان
دهان
یکی برنامده فریاد
فرو ریخته دندان‌ها همه،
سوتِ خارج‌خوانِ ترانه‌یِ روزگارانِ از یاد رفته
در وزشِ بادِ کهن
فرو نستاده هنوز
از کیِ باستان.

بادِ اعصارِ کهن در جمجمه‌هایِ روفته
بر ستونِ بی‌انتهایِ آهکین
فرو شده در ماسه‌هایِ انتظاریِ بدوی.

دفترهایِ سپیدِ بی‌گناهی
به تشتی چوبین
بر سر
معطل مانده بر دروازه‌یِ عبور:
نخِ پَرَکی چرکین
بر سوراخِ جوال‌دوزی.

اما خیال‌ات را هنوز
فراگردِ بسترم حضوری به کمال بود
از آن پیش‌تر که خواب‌ام به ژرفاهایِ ژرف اندرکشد.

گفتم اینک ترجمانِ حیات
تا قیلوله را بی‌بایست نپنداری.

Jagged and Endless...

Jagged and endless
spanning times past and yet to come,
skeletal columns
hollow sockets
bare ribs
a mouth
        swallowing its cry
teeth caved in
Off-key whistles linger
in the ancient wind
        echoing lost days
                of antiquity

Ancient winds through clean-swept skulls
on endless limestone columns
buried in the sands of primal longing

Blank notebooks of innocence
in a wooden tub
balanced on the head
waiting at the gate of passage—
a grimy thread
at the eye of a darning needle

But your presence
still surrounded my bed,
perfect and whole
before sleep pulled me
into its deepest depths

I thought, this is the meaning of life,
so don't take the midday rest for granted

آن‌گاه دانستم
که مرگ
پایان نیست.

۱۲ اسفندِ ۱۳۷۸

That's when I knew—
death
 is not the end

 March 2, 2000

Shamlou's autograph, inscribed in 1990 on a photo of us at our Tehran literary salon, circa 1982. From the Talebi family archives.

Notes to the Poems

Fog—In his *Collected Works*, Shamlou notes that *Golku* is a girl's name he first came across in a northern village. Likely a shortened form of *Golaku*, it combines *gol* (meaning "flower") with *ku*, a diminutive often used for girls. To Shamlou, *Golku* has the tender feel of a term of endearment.

From the Wound of Abaei's Heart—Aba Abaei (1921–1946), an Iranian Turkmen teacher and activist, was killed in August 1946 by Pahlavi police during a raid on a theater event organized by progressive artists in Gorgan. To bypass censorship at the time, the poem's title and references to Abaei in the poem were replaced with "Aman Jan," casting him as a legendary Turkmen hero.

Shamlou spent a great deal of time in Turkmen Sahra, a northeastern Iranian region along the Caspian Sea, known for its dramatic mountains, forests, and plains. The landscape left a deep mark on him, shaping the imagery in this poem. In a letter to a Turkmen admirer, he fondly recalled driving tractors across the endless plains, working long days in encampments, and sleeping in tents. He painted vivid scenes of rain, herds, regional fur hats, the distant howling of dogs, tireless women in bright dresses, fire pits sending up columns of smoke, and wild horses roaming free. In a note in his *Collected Works*, Shamlou recalled spotting a polite, modest man in a crowd, and only realizing it was Abaei when he heard him speak.

Shamlou traced the poem's origins to a sleepless night in a Turkmen tent. Across the fire pit, a young woman sat awake, her face lit by the flames. Earlier, Abaei had been mentioned, and when Shamlou asked if she knew him, she had remained silent. Seeing her awake late into the night, he imagined her thoughts were with Abaei. The sorrow in her almond-shaped eyes stayed with him, inspiring the poem a week later.

Nazli's Death—This poem honors Vartan Salakhanian (1931–1954), an Armenian-Iranian political activist arrested by the Pahlavi regime following the August 19, 1953 coup. Despite brutal torture, he refused to betray his comrades, ultimately dying when his captors drilled into his skull. His mutilated body was thrown into the Jajrud River and later recovered.

The 1953 Iranian coup d'état, known as Operation Ajax, was a covert operation orchestrated by the U.S. CIA and British MI6 to depose Iran's democratically elected Prime Minister, Mohammad Mosaddegh. The coup reinstated Shah Mohammad Reza Pahlavi, reversing Mosaddegh's nationalization of the Iranian oil industry. The pivotal event solidified the Shah's rule, ushered in an era of political repression, and set the stage for the 1979 Iranian Revolution.

Shamlou and Vartan were imprisoned at the same time. Shamlou briefly saw Vartan, whose body bore the scars of torture. The poem honors Vartan as a heroic martyr. To avoid censorship, Shamlou replaced Vartan's name with "Nazli," possibly to deflect attention, universalize the poem, or reference a nickname. The poem's original dedication, omitted in the *Collected Works*, has been restored here.

Common Love—The "dead of this year" refers to executed members of the Military Organization (سازمان نظامی), an intelligence network within the Tudeh Party of Iran (the Iranian Communist Party), also known as Tudeh Military Network, a covert intelligence arm of the Tudeh Party that had infiltrated the Iranian Armed Forces.

Paul Éluard was an important influence on Shamlou's poetry. Éluard's 1942 poem "Liberté," written during the German occupation of France—an excerpt of which appears here—seems to resonate strongly in both the tone of this poem and Shamlou's later poems, including "Edict."

>   Sur mes cahiers d'écolier
>   Sur mon pupitre et les arbres
>   Sur le sable de neige
>   J'écris ton nom
>   ...
>   Et par le pouvoir d'un mot
>   Je recommence ma vie
>   Je suis né pour te connaître
>   Pour te nommer
>
>   Liberté.
>
>   On my school notebooks
>   On my desk and on the trees
>   On the sand on the snow
>   I write your name
>   ...
>   And by the power of a word
>   I begin my life again
>   I was born to know you
>   To name you
>
>   Liberty.
>
>   [Translated by Samuel Beckett]

About Your Uncles—The final line refers to Morteza Keyvan (1921–1954), a literary critic, journalist, poet, and Tudeh Party member. He was arrested in September 1954—following the 1953 coup—for sheltering three Tudeh Military Network officers, and was executed for "treason" by firing squad on October 19, 1954 at Qasr prison in Tehran. Keyvan was a close friend of Shamlou, and the poem is dedicated to Shamlou's son, Siavoosh.

Fish—In the translation, I omitted the repeated openings "I think" and "I feel" that begin four stanzas in the original, as the English reads more directly and powerfully without them, while preserving the intent of the lines.

Epic!—The term *rend* (رند) is complex to translate into English, but briefly: Hafez used it to describe someone who rejects social conventions, who appears outwardly lewd, yet is inwardly upright and spiritually evolved. According to Mohammad-Reza Shafiei Kadkani, the *rend* is akin to a Nietzschean "superman," embodying the paradoxes of the human condition: free will and predestination, prayer and rebellion, asceticism and intoxication, sorrow and joy. The *rend* serves as an anti-establishment, counter-cultural figure and an irreligious alter-ego to Hafez's more respectable persona, providing a safeguard against the sanctimony of religious authorities.

I translated *rend* as "hustler" and "trickster," the latter an archetype most commonly represented by the Fool card in the Tarot deck: a paradoxical figure that signifies both innocence and wisdom, spontaneity and folly, beginnings and risk-taking. Like the *rend*, the trickster defies convention, challenges norms, and embarks on a journey of self-discovery, a liminal figure on a path toward transcendence.

Nocturnal (The Alleys are Tight)—Gohar-e Morad or Gohar Morad was the pen name of the Iranian writer, Gholam-Hossein Sa'edi (1936–1985).

Elegy—The poem commemorates Forough Farrokhzad (1934–1967), an influential Iranian poet and filmmaker known for her groundbreaking work that expanded Persian poetic themes and language. Her five volumes of poetry explored themes of love, individuality, and breaking societal norms, establishing her as a pioneering modernist and feminist voice in Persian literature. A passionate, often controversial figure, Farrokhzad also directed the acclaimed documentary *The House is Black*. Her life was cut tragically short in a car accident at age 32, yet her legacy as a cultural icon and literary innovator endures.

Letter—This poem, written in the classical *qasideh* form, is the only one whose structure I altered. I first translated it into a modern near-rhyming version, then condensed it into a prose summary, and finally settled on a middle path—maintaining the original cadences while allowing for a freer structure and avoiding forced rhyme.

This verse-letter, written in 1954 during Shamlou's imprisonment in Qasr prison, reflects a period of strained relations with his father after an argument months earlier at the Temporary Detention Center of the Police. To avoid political scrutiny, Shamlou backdated the letter to 1944, when he had been held for 21 months in a Russian-controlled Allied prison in Rasht. This deliberate misdating aimed to obscure its connection to Shamlou's post-1953 coup imprisonment, during which he refused to sign repentance letters initially denounced by the Tudeh Party but later endorsed to secure members' release. Disillusioned with both his fellow inmates and the party, Shamlou chose instead to compose this poignant poem.

When the manuscript of Blossoming in the Mist (1971) was submitted to the censorship bureau, the censor noted that, although the poem was dated 1944, the poem's themes and tone appeared to reference the political turmoil surrounding the 1953 coup.

The Simorgh, a benevolent bird in Persian mythology and literature, is believed to live high on the mysterious Mount Qaf, her feathers offering guidance and protection to those on spiritual quests.

Mas'ud Sa'd Salman (ca. 1046–1121) was a Persian poet associated with the Ghaznavid court who spent much of his life in and out of prison due to political intrigues. Renowned for his prison poems, he used his confinement to craft vivid, emotional verses reflecting solitude, nostalgia, and the stark realities of imprisonment, solidifying his legacy as a pioneer of this poetic genre in Persian literature.

Nocturnal (No, I Haven't Carved You)—The last stanza references the Quranic phrase kun fa-yakun (کُن فَیَکُونُ), which translates to "Be, and it is," signifying that when God wills something, it simply comes into existence by His command of "Be!".

Abraham in Flames—The collection of poems, Abraham in Flames, and its title poem draw from a post-biblical, apocryphal tale where Abraham, rejecting idolatry, destroys idols and declares his faith in one God. Enraged, King Nimrod orders him cast into a fire, but God miraculously makes the flames harmless. The story symbolizes faith, resistance to tyranny, and the redemption of those who uphold their truth.

The poem commemorates Mehdi Rezaei (1952–1972), a political activist and a member of the People's Mojahedin Organization of Iran. Following four years of revolutionary activities, he was executed by firing squad on September 7, 1972 at the Chitgar shooting grounds. Because of his youth, he became known as the Red Rose of the Revolution.

Esfandiar, a legendary Iranian hero from Ferdowsi's *Shahnameh* (*The Book of Kings*), was a prince of the Kayanian dynasty gifted with near invincibility by armor bestowed by Zarathustra. However, his eyes remained his sole vulnerability—his "Achilles' heel." Tasked by his father to defeat the hero Rostam in exchange for the throne, Esfandiar fell in battle when Rostam, guided by the mythical Simorgh, struck his eyes with a double-headed arrow crafted from a tamarisk branch and one of Simorgh's feathers. Before his death, Esfandiar forgave Rostam, blaming his fate on his father's ambition and the Simorgh's Arrow.

Nocturnal (You Didn't Just Happen to Me)—A *ghazal* is a traditional poetic form, similar to a sonnet, often expressing love, longing, or divine connection. It is typically composed of rhyming couplets with a recurring refrain. A *qasideh* (or *qasida*) is a longer, more formal ode-like poem, often used to praise, eulogize, or explore philosophical themes.

Edict—Iran Darroudi (1936–2021) was a world-renowned Iranian painter recognized for her unique style, often described as "dreamscapes."

Still I Think of That Raven—Esmaeil Khoei (1938–2021) was an Iranian poet and member of the Iranian Writers' Association. In his *Collected Works*, Shamlou clarifies that the reference to the valleys of Yush was not intended as a nod to his predecessor, poet Nima Yushij (whose name means from Yush). While parallels to Nima's isolation in modernizing Iranian poetry might be drawn, this was not Shamlou's intent.

Funeral Address—This poem was originally dedicated to Khosrow Rouzbeh (1915–1958), an Iranian military officer, mathematician, writer, and head of the Tudeh Party's military branch. Known for his radicalism and criticism of the party as too "moderate," Rouzbeh was captured in a shootout in July 1957, tried in secret, and executed at Qezel Qal'eh prison in May 1958. The night before, he wrote a seventy-page testament condemning capitalism and praising socialism. Defiant to the end, he refused a blindfold and shouted, "Long live the Tudeh Party of Iran! Long live Communism! Fire!" Shamlou later withdrew the dedication after learning of Rouzbeh's confession to assassinating five people, including journalist Mohammad Massoud.

The Chasm—The poem is dedicated to writer and journalist Khosrow Golesorkhi (1944–1974), renowned for his leftist and revolutionary poetry. Golesorkhi was arrested and charged with plotting to kidnap Crown Prince Reza Pahlavi. His military trial was broadcast live while Mohammad Reza Shah was hosting a Conference for Human Rights in Tehran. During the trial, Golesorkhi boldly condemned the court and was sentenced to death for his Marxist beliefs. He refused a blindfold, asked to face the red dawn, sang revolutionary songs to the end, and gave the command for his own execution at Chitgar.

Children of the Depths—Kaveh is a figure in Ferdowsi's tenth-century epic, *Shahnameh* (*The Book of Kings*). After losing several of his children to the serpent-shouldered king Zahhak, whose serpents' hunger could only be sated by a daily meal of two human brains, Kaveh refuses to surrender his last child to the king and raises his blacksmith's apron upon a spear as a standard of rebellion to lead the overthrow of the tyrant.

Distance (The Seventh "S")—The title refers to one of the seven symbolic items on the *Haft-Seen* (meaning "The Seven S's") altar, a centerpiece for Nowruz, the Persian New Year. Celebrated on the first day of spring, Nowruz marks the renewal of nature and has been observed for over 3,000 years across Iran, the Middle East, Central Asia, and beyond. The *Haft-Seen* display includes seven items, each beginning with the Persian letter س (S), representing growth, health, and prosperity. They are: Sabzeh (sprouts), Samanu (wheat pudding), Senjed (oleaster), Seer (garlic), Somaq (sumac), Serkeh (vinegar), and Seeb (apple).

I Can't Help But Be Beautiful—The poem's reference to an "imbecile" is an allusion to Ayatollah Khomeini.

Grappling with Silence—Shamlou occasionally referenced his pen name, Bamdad, in the poems, which I translate interchangeably as "Daybreak" (in this poem), or "Dawn" (in "Written in Dawn's Blood"), while at times preserving the original Persian (as in "At the Threshold").

In traditional Iranian architecture, *saqqakhaneh* (سقاخانه) refers to small public spaces built by locals or shopkeepers to offer water to passersby. These structures typically featured large stone basins filled with drinking water, with metal cups attached by chains. I've translated it as "mirrored fountain."

Khaneqah (خانقاه) refers to a Sufi lodge or retreat for spiritual practice, education, and communal gathering. Traditionally, spiritual seekers would pause and rest at one during their journeys. I've translated it as "mystics' shrine."

The Shamlou tribe, of Turkoman origin, was one of seven tribes that brought the Safavids to power, a dynasty that eventually fell due to stagnation, arrogance, and ignorance.

I've introduced the qualifier, *bazaari* (of the bazaar) to the phrase "beside a handful of bazaari basil/and a smashed onion" to evoke the mercantile undertone of the moment.

I Wasn't Born Yesterday—The poem's title, *Jakh-e Emrooz* (جخ امروز), is a colloquial Persian phrase. The word *jakh* (جخ) is an informal term meaning "just" or "only," adding emphasis to *emrooz* (امروز) meaning "today." Together, the phrase can translate to "just today" or "only today." The opening phrase aligns with the sentiment of the American idiom "I wasn't born yesterday," the phrase I've chosen to convey the spirit of the original phrase.

Rafidi is a derogatory nickname for a Shia Muslim who rejects the legitimacy of the early leaders recognized by the Sunni branch of Islam. The Qarmatians were a militant Isma'ili Shia movement.

And Then the Earth—Shamlou wrote part of this poem in the summer of 1964, but wanted to rethink it. That led to the poem "...And So Began the Ruin" (*Aida: Tree and Dagger and Memory!*). Twenty years later, he picked the poem back up.

Nelson Mandela—This poem was written a year before the South African anti-apartheid activist and politician was released from prison (February 11, 1990) after serving 27 years.

At the Threshold—*Bar-e Amanat* (بارِ امانت), translated as "The Burden of Trust," is a concept from the Quran (33:72) describing humanity's acceptance of a divine responsibility which the heavens, the earth, and the mountains declined. Often understood as free will and moral duty, it signifies the soul's unique role: carrying both the honor of divine trust and the weight of earthly trials. Sufi poets like Rumi and Hafez explore this theme, emphasizing the path toward spiritual knowledge and union with the Divine.

The Tale of Mahan's Restlessness—Shamlou's poetry collection, *The Tale of Mahan's Restlessness* (حدیثِ بی قراری ماهان), draws inspiration from the story of Mahan in the medieval Persian romance, *Haft Peykar* (*The Seven Portraits*—or sometimes *Seven Beauties*), by Nezami Ganjavi. Mahan succumbs to promises of pleasure from deceptive figures who reveal themselves as demons and cast him instead into barren deserts. Broken and humiliated by his failure to resist temptation, Mahan repents through pleas and tears and is eventually led home, deeply aware of the consequences of his misdeeds. His story is less a hero's journey than a cautionary tale about the perils of fleeting desires and the human struggle between spiritual integrity and worldly seductions. By invoking Mahan, Shamlou engages with themes of existential struggle and inner conflict. While Mahan did not seek enlightenment, his story resonates with Shamlou's meditations on the cost of surrendering to temptation.

Mahan's story echoes throughout the collection. In "Written in Dawn's Blood," Shamlou reflects on the omnipresence of death and frames survival and redemption as acts of creation, suggesting he transformed the brutalities of existence into art by inventing himself as Dawn. The closing poem, "Jagged and Endless," conjures the desolate landscapes of Mahan's journey as a metaphor for Shamlou's own restless confrontation with despair and resilience.

Reconciliation—This poem can be seen as a continuation of the poem "…And So Began the Ruin" (from *Aida: Tree and Dagger and Memory!*), and the poem "And Then the Earth…" (from *Unrewarded Eulogies*).

The Sixth Song—This poem can be seen as a continuation of "…And So Began the Ruin" (from *Aida: Tree and Dagger and Memory!*) and the poem "And Then the Earth…" (from *Unrewarded Eulogies*).

Those Who Stand Vigil in the Night—*Shab-e Qadr* (شبِ قدر), translated here as "Night of Destiny" (sometimes called "Night of Power"), is among the holiest nights in Islam, marking the Quran's initial revelation to the prophet Mohammad. Observed during the last ten nights of Ramadan, it is believed to bestow immense blessings, mercy, and forgiveness, while shaping an individual's destiny for the year ahead.

Written in Dawn's Blood—My translation of the title condenses the original phrase (با تخلّص خونین بامداد), which literally means "With the Bloody Pen Name of Dawn." This choice draws on the familiarity of the English phrase "Written in Blood." While "pen name" is omitted from the title for fluency, it remains in the poem's final line.

Patabeh (پاتابه), translated here as "boots," refers to protective leg wraps traditionally worn by shepherds, travelers, and sometimes soldiers in rough terrain. Made from cloth or leather, they provide support and guard against thorns and rocky ground. The English term "puttee" describes a similar type of wrap, particularly used by British and Indian military forces. However, while puttee carries strong military associations, *Patabeh* has a broader cultural role in the Persian tradition as practical leg protection.

General Note: Some dates may vary by one month or one year when converting the Solar Hijri calendar (which begins on or around March 21) to the Gregorian (which begins January 1). The two calendars differ by approximately 621 years.

Sources Consulted and Further Reading

Shamlou, Ahmad. *Majmou'e-ye Asar-e Ahmad Shamlou* [The Collected Works of Ahmad Shamlou]. Vol. 1. Tehran: Negah Publishing, 2004 (5th ed.); 2010 (9th ed.).

Mojabi, Javad. *Shenakhtnameh-ye Ahmad Shamlou* [Ahmad Shamlou Reader], 3rd ed. Tehran: Qatreh Publishing, 2002.

Mojabi, Javad. *Ayneh-ye Bamdad: Tanz o Hemaseh dar Asar-e Shamlou* [Bamdad's Mirror: Satire and Epic in Shamlou's Work]. Tehran: Behnegar Publications, 2011.

Salajegheh, Parvin. *Amirzadeh-ye Kashiha* [The Prince of Tiles]. Tehran: Morvarid Publications, 2005.

Alizadeh, Hossein and Seyed Mojtaba Zamiri. *Goft o Goo'i Sha'eraneh ba Bambad* [A Poetic Conversation with Bambad]. Tehran: Naghsh o Negar, 2001.

Atashi, Manouchehr. *Shamlou dar Tahlili Enteqadi* [Shamlou in Critical Analysis]. Tehran: Amitis Press, 2003.

Masih, Hiva, ed. *Ketab-e She'r: Ahmad Shamlou* [Book of Poetry: Ahmad Shamlou]. Compiled, corrected, and edited by Hiva Masih. Tehran: Qasidehsara Press, 2005.

Tikku, Girdhari, with Alireza Anushiravani. *A Conversation with Modern Persian Poets*. Costa Mesa, CA: Mazda Publishers, 2004.

Iranshahr Journal. Shamlou issue. Edited by Maliheh Tiregol. Ketab, October 2000.

Daftar-e Honar Journal. Shamlou issue. Edited by Bidjan Assadipour. 1997.

Encyclopaedia Iranica. "Hafez VIII. Hafez and Rendi." Edited by Ehsan Yarshater. Last modified December 15, 2002. Accessed March 10, 2025. https://www.iranicaonline.org/articles/hafez-viii.

"Mas'ud Sa'd Salman." *Golha Project*. Accessed March 10, 2025. https://www.golha.co.uk/en/people/666/masud-sad-salman.

Emami, Saber. "Hadis-e Biqarariyeh Mahan: Eshterak-e Daghdaghe'i Kamal-Yafteh Beyn-e Nezami Ganjavi va Ahmad Shamlou" [The Tale of Mahan's Restlessness: A Shared Perfected Concern Between Nezami

Ganjavi and Ahmad Shamlou]. *She'r Journal*, no. 32 (Summer 1382) 20–25. https://www.noormags.ir/view/fa/articlepage/201035/.

The Official Timeline prepared by Mrs. Aida Shamlou

Other English translations of Ahmad Shamlou's poetry include:

Shamlu, Ahmad. *Born Upon the Dark Spear: Selected Poems of Ahmad Shamlu*. Translated by Jason Bahbak Mohaghegh. New York: Contra Mundum Press, 2015.

Shamlu, Ahmad. *The Love Poems of Ahmad Shamlu*. Translated with an introduction and notes by Firoozeh Papan-Matin. Washington, D.C.: IBEX Publishers, 2005.

Shamlou, Ahmad. *77 Poems. Shamlou*. Translated by Saeed Saeedpoor. Tehran: Nika Publication, 2010.

Acknowledgments

If creativity thrives in the company we keep, this book is shaped by the brilliant minds who surrounded me. My Shamlou-inspired endeavors owe much to those who champion them. While I can't name everyone, a few stand out for their profound generosity and lasting impact on this selection:

My friend and attorney Eric Evans and his team proved the public domain status of Shamlou's works while providing sustained personal support. Saied Kazemi tirelessly guided me through Shamlou's oeuvre for over a decade, sharing insights that made this project possible. Translator and editor Lida Nosrati was irreplaceable as a sounding board, early reader, creative partner, sister-in-arms, and constant companion.

Poet and translator Alireza Abiz brought a critical perspective on my readings of the poems and lent his deep understanding of the nuances and challenges of translation, which shaped the authenticity of these renderings. Elizabeth T. Gray, Jr., another gifted poet and translator, enriched this project in its final stages with significant counsel and input. Dr. Farzaneh Doosti collaborated with me on comparing versions of the poems and prepared the Persian manuscript, ensuring its integrity. Dr. Aria Fani heaped enthusiasm and expertise.

I am deeply grateful to Mrs. Aida Shamlou, co-director of the Alef Bamdad Institute, for granting me the official worldwide rights to translate and publish Shamlou's works and for her stewardship of his literary estate. While Shamlou's writings are in the public domain in the United States and other English-speaking countries, her endorsement and authorization were invaluable. Her personal reflections brought depth and history to my projects, as did Solmaz Sepehri's and Alireza Abiz's efforts in facilitating key communications.

World Poetry Books' Matvei Yankelevich anchored the project with creative freedom, thoughtful guidance, and a spirit of joy. The insights of his reading team, especially Roz Shayan Naimi, helped shape the translations.

This work owes much to my parents' steadfast protection of my time and space, shielding me during its most demanding final two years—a gift of immeasurable sacrifice.

I am grateful for a 2024 National Endowment for the Arts Literary Translation Fellowship, which provided crucial support in the final stages. Earlier sponsors (2013–2019) supported the project's initial phases, during which early versions of these translations appeared in *Self-Portrait in Bloom* (l'Aleph, 2019)—my memoir and literary portrait of Shamlou—and helped fund our operatic project, *Abraham in Flames* (World Premiere, 2019). Writers' residencies at Ledig House, La Maison de Beaumont, and Rebel Mountain Farms provided the solitude and space I needed.

Finally, I thank the editors of *Los Angeles Review of Books, Caesura Magazine, Critical Flame, Aster(ix) Journal, Consequence Magazine, Parsagon: The Persian Literature Review, Hafteh,* and *The Markaz Review,* as well as the reviewers of *San Francisco Classical Voice, San Francisco Chronicle, Mercury News, OperaWire, Parterre Box, Hyperallergic, The Rumpus, World Literature Today, Mizan,* and *Hannah Terry Blog,* among many others who published, discussed, and celebrated these translations alongside my broader body of work.

For Freedom.

Ahmad Shamlou, ca. 1960s.
Photograph by Hadi Shafaieh.

One of the most influential cultural figures of Iran in the latter half of the twentieth century, **Ahmad Shamlou** (1925–2000) authored more than 70 books, including 18 volumes of poetry. Sometimes known by his pen name, Alef Bamdad, Shamlou's innovations brought on a transition from classical forms to free verse and made him a flag-bearer of the Iranian vanguard, which included the poet Forough Farrokhzad. Shamlou's synthesis of Eastern and Western poetic traditions and high and low styles democratized the literary mode without simplifying it. Championing the "everyman," Shamlou's work reflects his deep engagement with social issues and the human condition.

Niloufar Talebi is an author, translator, and interdisciplinary artist. She has spent most of the past two decades working on projects related to Ahmad Shamlou. *Elegies of the Earth* is part of this suite of projects that includes the memoir *Self-Portrait in Bloom* (l'Aleph), an opera (*Abraham in Flames*, with composer A. Vrebalov), the video-poem *Funeral Address*, and a TEDx Talk. Talebi is the editor and translator of *Belonging: New Poetry by Iranians Around the World* (North Atlantic Books), and her multimedia projects include *ICARUS/ RISE*, *The Persian Rite of Spring*, *Fire Angels*, *The Plentiful Peach*, and *Epiphany*. Talebi is a Fulbright Scholar, and the recipient of translation prizes including a National Endowment for the Arts Translation Fellowship for her translations of Shamlou's poetry.

The Persian in this book was typeset in IRLotus, an Iranian modification of Linotype Lotus Arabic. The English was typeset in Nassim, a multi-script typeface family designed by Titus Nemeth for Rosetta Type Foundry, Brno. Cover design by Andrew Bourne. Typesetting by Don't Look Now. Printed and bound in Lithuania by BALTO Print. Manufactured by Arctic Paper in Sweden, the paper in this book meets EU Ecolabel, Forest Stewardship Council, and Cradle to Cradle certification standards.

 WORLD POETRY

Samer Abu Hawwash
Ruins and Other Poems
tr. Huda J. Fakhreddine

Marie-Noëlle Agniau
The Escapades
tr. Jesse Hover Amar

Nadia Anjuman
Smoke Drifts:
Selected Poems
tr. Diana Arterian
& Marina Omar

Jean-Paul Auxeméry
Selected Poems
tr. Nathaniel Tarn

Leire Bilbao
Fish Scales: Selected Poems
tr. Joana Urtasun

Boethius
The Poems from On the
Consolation of Philosophy
tr. Peter Glassgold

Maria Borio
Transparencies
tr. Danielle Pieratti

Astrid Cabral
Spotlight on the Word
tr. Alexis Levitin

Jeannette L. Clariond
Goddesses of Water
tr. Samantha Schnee

Jacques Darras
John Scotus Eriugena
at Laon
tr. Richard Sieburth

Mario dell'Arco
Day Lasts Forever:
Selected Poems
tr. Marc Alan Di Martino

Marie de Quatrebarbes
The Vitals
tr. Aiden Farrell

Ricardo Domeneck
First Epistle to the
Amphibians: Selected Poems
tr. Chris Daniels

Olivia Elias
Chaos, Crossing
tr. Kareem James Abu-Zeid

Gastón Fernández
Apparent Breviary
tr. KM Cascia

Jerzy Ficowski
Everything I Don't Know
tr. Jennifer Grotz
& Piotr Sommer
PEN AWARD FOR POETRY IN TRANSLATION

Antonio Gamoneda
Book of the Cold
tr. Katherine M. Hedeen &
Víctor Rodríguez Núñez

Mireille Gansel
Soul House
tr. Joan Seliger Sidney

Óscar García Sierra
Houston, I'm the problem
tr. Carmen Yus Quintero

Phoebe Giannisi
Homerica
tr. Brian Sneeden

Zuzanna Ginczanka
On Centaurs & Other Poems
tr. Alex Braslavsky

Julien Gracq
Abounding Freedom
tr. Alice Yang

Karmelo C. Iribarren
You've Heard This One
Before: Selected Poems
tr. John R. Sesgo

Leeladhar Jagoori
What of the Earth
Was Saved
tr. Matt Reeck

Nakedness Is My End:
Poems from the Greek
Anthology
tr. Edmund Keeley

Birhan Keskin
Earthly Conditions:
Selected Poems
tr. Öykü Tekten

Jazra Khaleed
The Light That Burns Us
ed. Karen Van Dyck

Judith Kiros
O
tr. Kira Josefsson

Dimitra Kotoula
The Slow Horizon
That Breathes
tr. Maria Nazos

Maria Laina
Hers
tr. Karen Van Dyck

Maria Laina
Rose Fear
tr. Sarah McCann

Perrin Langda
A Few Microseconds on
Earth
tr. Pauline Levy Valensi

Anna Malihon
Girl with a Bullet
tr. Olena Jennings

Afrizal Malna
Document Shredding
Museum
tr. Daniel Owen

Joyce Mansour
In the Glittering Maw:
Selected Poems
tr. C. Francis Fisher

Manuel Maples Arce
Stridentist Poems
tr. KM Cascia

Selma Meerbaum-Eisinger
Song of the Yellow Asters
tr. Carlie Hoffman

Ennio Moltedo
Night
tr. Marguerite Feitlowitz

Meret Oppenheim
The Loveliest Vowel Empties:
Collected Poems
tr. Kathleen Heil

Giovanni Pascoli
Last Dream
tr. Geoffrey Brock
RAIZISS/DE PALCHI
TRANSLATION AWARD

Gabriel Pomerand
Saint Ghetto of the Loans
tr. Michael Kasper &
Bhamati Viswanathan

Liliana Ponce
Theory of the Voice and Dream
tr. Michael Martin Shea

Rainer Maria Rilke
Where the Paths Do Not Go
tr. Burton Pike

Amelia Rosselli
Document
tr. Roberta Antognini
& Deborah Woodard

Elisabeth Rynell
Night Talks
tr. Rika Lesser

Waly Salomão
Border Fare
tr. Maryam Monalisa Gharavi

George Sarantaris
Abyss and Song:
Selected Poems
tr. Pria Louka

George Seferis
Book of Exercises II
tr. Jennifer R. Kellogg
ELIZABETH CONSTANTINIDES
MEMORIAL TRANSLATION PRIZE

Seo Jung Hak
The Cheapest France in Town
tr. Megan Sungyoon

Ahmad Shamlou
Elegies of the Earth:
Selected Poems
tr. Niloufar Talebi

Edith Södergran
Modern Woman
tr. CD Eskilson

Ardengo Soffici
Simultaneities &
Lyric Chemisms
tr. Olivia E. Sears

Liesl Ujvary
Good & Safe
tr. Ann Cotten &
Anna-Isabella Dinwoodie

Paul Verlaine
Before Wisdom:
The Early Poems
tr. Keith Waldrop
& K.A. Hays

Haris Vlavianos
Renaissance
tr. Patricia Barbeito

Witold Wirpsza
Apotheosis of Music
tr. Frank L. Vigoda

Uljana Wolf
kochanie, today i bought bread
tr. Greg Nissan

Ye Lijun
My Mountain Country
tr. Fiona Sze-Lorrain

Verónica Zondek
Cold Fire
tr. Katherine Silver